Self
and Family

CHOICES

GUIDES FOR TODAY'S WOMAN

Self
and Family

Jane Cary Peck

The Westminster Press
Philadelphia

Scripture quotations from the Revised Standard
Version of the Bible are copyrighted 1946, 1952, ©
1971, 1973 by the Division of Christian Education
of the National Council of the Churches of Christ in
the U.S.A. and are used by permission.

Book design by Alice Derr

First edition

Published by The Westminster Press ®
Philadelphia, Pennsylvania

PRINTED IN THE UNITED STATES OF AMERICA
9 8 7 6 5 4 3 2 1

Library of Congress Cataloging in Publication Data

Peck, Jane Cary, 1932–
    Self and family.

    (Choices : guides for today's woman ; no. 11)
    Bibliography: p.
    1. Family. 2. Wives. 3. Mothers. 4. Sex role.
5. Self. I. Title. II. Series: Choices ; 11.
HQ734.P34 1984   306.8′5   84-13166
ISBN 0-664-24547-1 (pbk.)

Dedicated
with love

to my family

Bob
Bob, Jim, Cary Liisa, and Jonathan Thanh Danh

and especially
to my mother

Ruth Moran Chapman

CONTENTS

I FAMILY AND SOCIETY

1. The Nature and Functions of the Family   13
2. Qualities and Issues of Family Life   32
3. Social Witness of the Family   47

II WOMEN IN FAMILY LIFE

4. Becoming a Woman-Self in the Family   57
5. Self and Marriage   66
6. Self and Children   89

BIBLIOGRAPHY   117

PUBLISHER'S ACKNOWLEDGMENT

The publisher gratefully acknowledges the advice of several distinguished scholars in planning this series. Virginia Mollenkott, Arlene Swidler, Phyllis Trible, and Ann Ulanov helped shape the goals of the series, identify vital topics, and locate knowledgeable authors. Views expressed in the books, of course, are those of the individual writers and not of the advisers.

PART I

Family and Society

CHAPTER 1

The Nature
and Functions of the Family

Women today are facing uncertainties brought about by changes in society and changing family roles; women are also striving to effect many of these changes. Because of the changing society, there are pressures on the family. And because the family is changing—indeed, is in transition—there is sometimes panic and at other times excitement and vital interest on the part of family members, especially women. Yet while specific individual families experience stress from change very directly, the particular family isn't responsible for these changes and has little influence over them; the stress is societal.

As Christian family women and churchwomen facing social stresses in and on the family and ourselves, how are we dealing with these changes? Do we have a specific responsibility or opportunity in relation to the family and to society? What is our perspective on the family today?

Our society has many ideas and assumptions about the family that need to be examined. First, what *is* the family? It exists everywhere, but in multiple forms, and it has changed since our grandparents' day—and even more so before that. Second, what are the *functions* of the family? The things a family does for its members and the wider society can be examined, starting from our own point of expertise: What is *your* experience of the family, and, concretely, how is family life—in whatever form—working for you? How do you see the relationship between your selfhood and your family life? Is the family for you an arena for the realization of your gifts and a support for using your gifts for ministry in the world? Third, the family is also in relationship with the wider society. How would you describe this relationship on the basis of your own experience and that of other families you know?

These questions set the context for our consideration of today's family life as lived, evaluated, and challenged by churchwomen endeavoring to be responsible in their faith.

UNDERSTANDING A FAMILY

What do we mean by the term "family"? The answer to that question may seem obvious: husband-father, wife-mother, and children—in other words, the nuclear family—living separately from other people in their own house or apartment, the most important people in one another's lives. In this conventional picture, the nuclear family is organized around a division of labor between women and men seen as being based on biology, with men playing the role of breadwinner, provider, and protector and women playing the role of housekeeper and emotional mainstay, one of whose major functions is to care for and socialize children. Often when we talk about "the family," this is what we have in mind; we assume that the family *is* the nuclear family, that this has always been the form of the family, and that it has always operated with the same roles and functions.

HISTORICAL PERSPECTIVE

In fact, however, this form of the family is a fairly recent development. Until two or three hundred years ago, the separate nuclear family did not exist. People lived together across family and age lines and social class: large extended families plus servants and workers. There was little distinction of conjugal units of parents and children. Children were regarded as small adults and participated as such in the work of the whole group, often being sent away from their own parents at age seven or eight to work for years as apprentices or servants on other estates; childhood did not exist. Nor did privacy exist: people were together day and night, all rooms opened into each other, and people slept in all rooms of the dwelling place, servants and masters together. Everyone participated in the common work, dwelling place and workplace were identical, and all—women, men, children—were engaged in labor.

Only after the Middle Ages did a separate period of childhood develop; children began to be distinguished from adults, and parents began to attend to their education. In the eighteenth century, the middle-class family home became smaller, private, separate from society; only a married couple and their children lived together, while servants and workers and extra relatives moved into separate residences. The modern home was developed, with the privacy of rooms opening onto corridors instead of into each other and the distinction of rooms with separate functions (sleeping, cooking-and-eating, or receiving visitors). Only in the last century did this middle-class family pattern become common for all of society. (See Philippe Ariès; the full reference for this citation and others is given in the Bibliography.)

With the development of industrialism, the family lost most economic functions and became private. A specialized place devoted to work was invented: the factory. The workers—men and lower-class women and many children—left their traditional domain and daily went off to work in another place, a very different environment from their home. Thus the workers' lives became split between job and family, while those who didn't go off to work (some women and children and the elderly) were concerned only with family life.

This division of space into work areas and living areas represents a striking change, a division into public and private spheres, with the family falling within the private. With this change, the family became more removed from the community, withdrew into itself, and even came to be rather hostile to the external world; it became *the* private domain, the only place a person could go to escape the view and regulation of industrial society. In the workplace, workers were subject to constant surveillance, whereas the family home was a place of refuge, free of outside control and much more conducive to emotional expression than the working world.

A sexual division of labor accompanied this division of life into public and private spheres, with men going away from home to work and women staying at home to take care of the house and children; motherhood became a full-time occupation—for those in the middle and upper classes who could afford it. The main functions of the family became providing intimacy and long-term child nurture.

The family thus changed as a social institution, *becoming* in our recent history the private, nuclear family we are apt to assume it has been throughout history.

FAMILY FORMS

But in our day many of us know or are part of families that are not nuclear families; therefore, the common assumption that "the family" is the nuclear family does not match present reality. As we hear all the time, the nuclear family is declining: In 1970, nuclear families represented 40.3 percent of all U.S. households, while by 1980 they were only 32.4 percent. The divorce rate in the United States more than doubled between 1963 and 1975, and in the decade from 1971 to 1981 the number of divorced people increased from 47 to 109 of every 1,000 married persons. (The divorce rate per 1,000 married persons for black Americans increased to 233; for Hispanics, 110; and for whites, 100.) Of particular concern to women is the fact that there are over 4 million displaced homemakers: 75 percent of these women are over 40, 65 percent are economically disadvantaged, and 25 percent are minority women. After a divorce, women are less likely to remarry than men, and they remarry less quickly. In 1980, women headed 15 percent of U.S. families, and this 15 percent was *half of all poor families in the country.* Twenty percent of all children now live in one-parent families, an increase of 53.9 percent since 1970; divorce is the primary reason. Ninety percent of these children live with their mothers, and although the number living with their fathers has increased by 61 percent in the last ten years, more children live with other relatives than with their fathers.

Is the family dying? These figures might make it seem so, and with especially detrimental effects for women and children. But besides nuclear and single-parent families, there are other types of households: the couple (wife and husband with no children at home), the nuclear family reconstituted by remarriage, a kin network (three-generation household or extended family), experimental households (commune-type family groupings), unrelated people living together, gay and lesbian partners with or without children, unmarried heterosexual couples, and single individuals without children. The last two types have increased dramatically in recent

years. Two-person households of unmarried people living with a member of the opposite sex more than tripled
in number in the past decade: from 523,000 in 1970 to
1,808,000 in 1981. And the number of people living
alone has increased by 75 percent since 1970: About 23
percent of all adults live singly, and about one of every
five U.S. households is a one-person household.

Some of these other types of households are also families. So while the nuclear family is declining, the family
is not disappearing but continuing, in a greater variety
of forms than most of us realize.

If we consider the different families we know in our
own experience, we can recognize this for ourselves. I
can think of the following forms and examples of family
structure:

1. Nuclear/conjugal family (married couple with children)
   a. Isolated or embedded in a network of relatives
   b. Children born to or adopted by the parents
      • My own family: wife, husband, and four chil-
        dren, two of whom are adopted and two of
        whom are adults living away from home; we live
        very far away from most close relatives
2. Reconstituted nuclear family (second marriage for
   one or both partners, with children from previous
   marriages)
      • Elaine, a divorced doctor recently remarried,
        shares custody of her little daughter with her ex-
        husband, a professor in the same town
      • Ruth and her two teenagers live with her sec-
        ond husband, whose young son by a previous
        marriage visits them each summer
3. Married couple without children, or none living at
   home
      • In my church as I grew up, Charles, married late

to Gertrude and without children, was adored
by all us kids for playing with us on the church
lawn after the worship service

4. One-parent family (mother or father with children)
    - Sue is a pastor, recently divorced, with two teen-
      agers who live with her in the parsonage
    - Working in a day-care center, Sharon is off wel-
      fare but barely able to feed and house her fam-
      ily of three children
    - Liz, a divorced seminary student, entertains her
      son when he comes on weekend visits from his
      home with his father

5. Extended family
    a. Nuclear family with additional relatives living to-
       gether
       - My husband's family for some years had a cousin
         and her daughter living in the household with
         his parents, his two brothers, and himself
       - My aunt, widowed when her second child was
         nine months old, raised her children in the
         home of her aunt and uncle, who had no chil-
         dren
    b. Single-parent household that includes other rela-
       tives
       - Betty's household includes her two children, an
         elderly uncle, and a second cousin who is in col-
         lege

6. Heterosexual committed relationship (unmarried
   conjugal relationship between a woman and a man,
   with or without children)
    - Margaret, a professional woman, shares a long-
      term committed relationship with a man in the
      same profession in another city

7. Homosexual committed relationship (gay or lesbian
   couple, with or without children)
    - Rachel is a writer, long divorced, who has raised

her thirteen-year-old son alone until the past three years, when she entered a committed relationship with Lisa, a school band director; the three live together as a family

8. Communal family (intentionally created family of unrelated individuals or a combination of unrelated and related persons sharing a household)
   - A communal household committed to religious peace action is made up of Brad, Meg, and their baby; Cynthia and Sam and their infant; and Helen, a single woman

All these are forms of families, and Wilson Yates defines "family" broadly to include them all: "The family is a kinship unit of two or more persons who are related by marriage, blood, primary commitment, or adoption and who usually share a common culture and common residence" ("The Family and Power"). Thus, while the signs of strain and decline of the family are evident and some people fear for its survival, Professor Yates and others believe that the family has a future and that the shape this future is taking is the emergence of a new pluralism of forms and styles alongside the nuclear family.

FUNCTIONS OF THE FAMILY

Recognizing, then, that the family as the basic human community comes in all shapes and sizes, and still thinking about its health and survival, let us now ask, What does the family actually *do* for people? Sociologists may answer with a list of basic functions the family performs for its members:

- Provides a context for sexual relations, reproduction, and nurturance and socialization of children
- Provides social status and economic support

- Provides emotional nurturance of adult members

Reproduction. Many of these functions are being challenged in today's society by social changes: changing sex roles, contraceptive technology, high mobility, industrialization, and so on. Marriage is no longer the expected life-style for all; many women and men are choosing to remain single, as we have seen in the statistics given earlier. And marriage is no longer the only socially acceptable context for sexual relations, or even reproduction or child rearing: couples engage in sexual relations outside marriage, as some always have done, but now openly live together; single women give birth, by choice or circumstance, and single women and men adopt children and then raise children as single parents. Other couples are choosing not to have children or to have only one. Day-care centers and schools now share significantly in the nurturance and socialization of children.

Social and economic status and support. Social status is increasingly achieved by individuals, based on their work, not acquired automatically at birth (based on "good family" or the opposite). And the economic function of the family has changed: Until the end of the last century, marriage was an economic necessity for our grandparents and great-grandparents, who were mutually dependent on each other; the household was a family enterprise of completely intermingled productive and maintenance functions, husband and wife and children all working together on the family farm or store. Later, when home and work became separate places, men went away to earn money as "providers" while women stayed at home as "homemakers," and women and children became dependent on men for economic support. From being a cooperative economic union, marriage became a dependent economic union for women, often an economic necessity for them but not for men. (Now that more women are earning incomes from outside employment, this economic function of marriage is changing to some extent but not totally.) The primary economic activity of the family is no longer production but consumption.

Emotional nurturance. We see that some traditional functions of the family are changing. However, emotional nurturance of adult family members, though met partially outside the family in various organizations and friendships, is still largely provided in the family, and especially in marriage. This is a key pull toward family life. As social beings, most humans prefer to live in community with a partner, child, or close friend or relative, within a family as a deep context for human closeness in long-term supportive intimacy. Besides this human pull toward intimate community, people today feel pushed toward marriage, in particular, by the stressful nature of our society. Some scholars conclude that people in industrialized countries of the developed world feel the need for marriage especially *because of* the strains of the economic and political system. Many women need marriage as a context for human closeness, but most also for economic survival, while men need marriage as a source of identity and self-respect against the alienating pressures of the workplace: its stress, tension, frustration, and lack of satisfaction. Society expects the nuclear family to provide support and comfort against the emotional stress created by the industrial system. Comforting and consuming may now be the two primary functions of the modern family! The family is expected to provide emotional solace, particularly to men. As our society becomes more complex, mobile, and rootless, people have less access to supportive relatives and friends in their daily lives, and especially their work. Yet emotional demands for intimacy, nurturance, and personal acceptance are actually increased by our complex, bureaucratic, industrialized social system. Our society offers few opportunities besides the family to satisfy these emotional demands.

Some psychologists find that family health, happiness, and stability are mainly dependent on the stability of the human networks surrounding the family, and in our society this is largely determined by economics. The family does not exist in isolation, however much we retreat into the privacy of our separate homes and try to be self-sufficient. We exist in society, and society plays a big role both in determining what the family's functions are and how it performs them.

PRESSURES ON THE FAMILY

Family systems usually reflect the environmental stress and strain of the age in which they exist. Most of us have experienced in our own lives at least some pressure or influence from society that makes it harder to raise our children the way we believe in, harder to keep our marriages together, harder to get and keep jobs to support our families, harder to live when far away from our children and grandchildren or our old circle of friends. It is even more difficult to survive against social conditions such as racism that hamper us in nearly everything we do, against physical abuse from husbands that we're afraid to report, against arson that burns down our apartment building. We know what unemployment, or frequent moves to find or keep work, or the mass media, can do to family life and values. Let's look at some of these pressures from society.

WORK-RELATED PROBLEMS

Basically, people are unsettled about the family to-day. Family functions have changed, work has changed, women have gone out of the home to work, families are more independent from extended families and more dependent on the economic system. Many of the unsettling problems of the family are work-related, and particularly related to women's work.

Unemployment. One of the most difficult problems of the family is finding work. Unemployment undercuts the ability of the family to support itself, undercuts self-esteem, hurts children's health and therefore their ability to learn, seriously threatens marriages, contributes to physical abuse in the home, and may even lead to suicide.

The traditional responsibility for child care borne by women is related to both unemployment and underemployment. One of every five or six unemployed women is jobless because she has no alternative child care. Further, women are overrepresented in part-time work compared to men, because they must combine child care with work in the labor force. Though part-time work outside the home may be desirable for some women for just this reason, for others, both the unavailability of adequate child care and the unavailability of full-time paid employment present serious problems.

We women work for the same reasons as men, chiefly to support ourselves and our families or to contribute to their support; one third of the women in the labor force are the sole supporters of their families. Thus, unemployment and underemployment of women are serious problems for us and our families, as is unemployment and underemployment of men who are husbands and fathers.

Income. Adequate income from work is also a job-related problem for women and their families. This may involve both child-care costs and racial discrimination. In general, women who work outside the home retain primary responsibility for household tasks and child care, thus increasing the amount of overall stress, limiting upward mobility (since higher-paying jobs usually require more time and energy), and locking women into lower-paying jobs. Traditional sex roles contribute to less adequate incomes for family women. Racism results in lower pay for both women and men of minority families.

Women's poverty. Poverty is both a women's problem and a racial problem, and poor families are a children's issue. In 1978 there were 1.2 million *fewer* poor children in families headed by men than in 1968, but 1.5 million *more* in families headed by women. The poverty rate of families headed by women is triple that of other families. If this rate continues, by the year 2000 almost all people living in poverty will be single women or family members supported by women!

But the problem of poverty for working women is made even worse by racial discrimination. In 1980 the median incomes for women who worked full-time, year-round, and were heads of households were:

White women	$16,988
Hispanic women	13,337
Black women	13,214

The figures for the median income of *all* female-headed families (including women who do not work outside the home and those who work full-time and part-time) are, of course, lower for each racial group:

White women	$11,908
Black women	7,425
Hispanic women	7,031

We've already seen that the 15 percent of U.S. families headed by women made up *half* of all poor families in the country in 1980. And we can see that adequate income is an even greater problem for women of color. Thus, poverty is a women's issue, a racial issue, and a children's issue—and one of the most significant pressures on the family today.

Job pressures and dissatisfactions. A problem for those who have jobs is the emotional toll of high-powered jobs and of jobs with little satisfaction, and the resulting drain on the family. There is a lot of psychological tension in the high-powered jobs of our present industrial system, with their pressures of competition and unlimited requirements for performance and expectations of achievement. These jobs demand that high-level employees keep on their toes every minute. This psychological burden falls especially on men, who hold the vast majority of these jobs in every field. A different kind of emotional toll is taken by lower-level jobs in which there is little job satisfaction or which require high-speed, repetitious work.

Mobility. One of the reasons the family is under stress is its mobility. The high mobility of families is a result primarily of requirements of work. Families have to move, sometimes frequently, when the wage earner is transferred, gets a better job, or finds a job after being unemployed. This is regular policy in some companies and is common in the military and in government service and some university departments. It is frequent in the case of moving up the ladder in business. And in these days of high unemployment, people find themselves willing to move almost anywhere in desperation for work. The result of this mobility, for whatever reason, is dislocation, disruption, and isolation of the family.

Conventional family assumed. Work is structured on the basis of the conventional family: husband-father out in the world as wage earner and wife-mother at home with children and housework as homemaker. The assumption of the workplace is that wage earners are free to give exclusive attention to their jobs because of the support work of child care, food preparation, and cleaning by homemakers. Some jobs literally assume that work at home will be performed by the wage earner's wife, such as the entertaining of clients, prospects, or diplomats and other visitors from overseas. Some corporations interview the wives of candidates for an executive position to determine their suitability for what the business expects of them. This assumption is made even clearer now that women are being hired for some executive jobs: they don't quite fit in a number of ways, one of which is that they don't have wives to entertain for them.

Women working outside the home. Part of the reason people are unsettled about the family today is the question of women's work. Since the structure of work assumes the conventional family, when women work outside the home, there is stress on both them and their families. Their jobs, like men's, assume the presence of a wife at home providing all the support work to enable full-time, undivided attention to the paid employment, uninterrupted by snow days, taking sick children to the doctor, or an absent baby-sitter. These women are not available, or are not *as* available, for professional entertaining for their husbands and may have to do their own such entertaining. Availability of time and emotional energy for soothing a husband's frayed nerves may be sharply decreased by a woman's own work stress or even enthusiasm for some work project. And women may not be as available for their children, for chauffeuring to lessons and friends, making cookies for Cub Scouts or attending the open session of dance lessons, or helping with homework and giving snacks after school.

It is overwhelmingly true that women work a double shift when they work outside the home, doing the paid job at their workplace and then continuing to do most of the housework as well. Studies have shown that husbands of women who work outside the home do only about an hour more of housework per week than husbands of women who are full-time homemakers, though these men express willingness and a sense of responsibility for doing more than they actually do. Family lifestyles and sex roles do not necessarily change when women take jobs.

ISOLATION OF HOUSEHOLD

The modern family is isolated from other people, and from the life of society, in private homes and even specialized residential areas called suburbs. Within these separate residences, women and young children live apart from the rest of society. Young mothers often feel cut off from their former life, their families and friends and perhaps their work and social life. Alone with their infants and preschoolers, they miss the stimulation and companionship of adults. For some of us, the experience of postpartum distress resulted at least in part from the isolation we found ourselves in when we returned from the hospital with our babies; this is in sharp contrast to previous generations and to other cultures in which new mothers are still surrounded by other women and supported by their experience.

Housework too—meal preparation, clothes washing, cleaning—is carried out by millions of isolated individuals when these tasks could be done better and more humanely as communal work. And married couples themselves are separated by the split of home and work: wives stay in the privacy of the home, while their husbands participate in both private and public realms.

Our culture promotes privacy and the rights of the family and the separation of the private realm from the public. It upholds the higher morality and greater humanity of the private arena. And it generally puts women, and the church, in charge of maintaining these higher values for the good of society.

QUESTIONING THE ROLE OF THE FAMILY AND ROLES *IN* THE FAMILY

SOCIAL ROLE OF THE FAMILY

Can the family fulfill society's expectations for humanizing modern life, when it itself lacks support and is in transition, undergoing change, stressed by such things as mobility, economic hardship, and racism? *Should* the family be expected to bind up the wounds of its members so that they can continue to function in and serve the needs of industrialized society? Isn't this too heavy a burden, an emotional overload on the family and particularly on women? The isolated family cannot compensate for the toll taken by work and the structure and pace of modern society; the weak private realm cannot make up for the human cost of the dominant public realm. Is this something we family women might talk about earnestly together, since we are expected to be the mainstay of family life? We encounter pressure from so-

ciety, church, husbands, older relatives—even ourselves—to stay at home, support the family, and provide
this needed nurturing nest. But even if we do, *can* the
family carry the burden expected by society? And
should it? Or should society be changed—as to either
the nature and requirements of work or the isolation of
families or both—so as not to exact so high a cost from
human beings? It seems to me that family women can
and should be leaders in raising these questions and dis-
cussing them.

AUTONOMY OF THE FAMILY

How much power does the family have over its own
destiny? How much can it shape its own form and style?
To a certain extent the family can work to improve the
quality of its relationships, reshape sex roles of wife and
husband, move from a more traditional to a more equal
spousal relationship and a less authoritarian pattern of
child rearing; or it can socialize children in particular
political and economic and religious values, determine
its own size; and spouses can divorce. The family *can*
make some choices, and the more intentional it is about
this decision making, the greater its ability to deal with
the changes it is experiencing. Yet even these internal
decisions are affected by society. For example:

- A family trying to reach sex-role equality or limit
  TV watching is in conflict with the dominant culture and mostly without support or social models
- Relationships suffering because of economic or
  racist social conditions can't be improved simply
  by goodwill within the family

Our society is highly organized and interdependent;
everything is done within institutions. Therefore, none
of our social institutions can be independent or isolated,
least of all marriage and the family.

I am arguing that the family cannot realize its full potential in our present cultural environment, despite the degree of power available to it. Another social institution, the church, could and does, to some extent, serve as a supporting institution for the family, mediating between it and the rest of society and enhancing its power.

Both family and church have power to act *on* society; they can take positive initiatives to influence society on behalf of the family's own needs and to bring about change in dehumanizing social conditions. One of the most appropriate foci for such intentional change action is the intersection of family and work. Instead of taking away women's traditional home roles as the price of allowing women into the public world, we can strive for the reintegration of home and work, open up home roles to the participation of men, and struggle to retain home values in the public world. This would change the public world at least to some extent with these values, involving significant social reconstruction: home and work in closer proximity, child care at or near the workplace, more flexible work schedules, resocialization of isolated individual homes, and racial and economic justice.

This would represent a radical change from the family's generally passive and dependent role in our society today. In order to strengthen the family and preserve its values, the family would take an active role for social change, in the face of enormous obstacles of the present social structure. I am recognizing here that the family can act as a moral agent.

CHAPTER 2

Qualities and Issues of Family Life

Family units are both psychological units, with meshing patterns of human relationships, and economic units, usually sharing housing, meals, and other necessities bought by money.

In both dimensions the most common model in the public mind is the nuclear family, and my discussion will often seem most applicable to this unit. Nevertheless, other types of families share similar qualities and issues. In the same way, causes of dissolution and enrichment are comparable in conventional marriages and other forms of families.

PERSONAL RELATIONSHIPS

Closeness of people, physically and emotionally, is an important component of families.

PARTNERSHIP

Particularly in families where there is more than one adult, partnership is vital. It is important that this be a relationship of mutuality and a communion of equals, a companionship. How deeply soul-satisfying it is for humans, who are social beings by nature and who long for community, to be companions.

But for some, companionship and equality pose a threat. Certainly this understanding, particularly of marriage, isn't traditional. In the past several generations and in some present religious interpretations of Scripture, the assumption was that the husband is dominant, the head of the family, and the wife his helpmate, secondary and submissive; and such positions have been given religious value. Today some religious spokespersons assert that this secondary status is women's religious duty. Tasks and roles have been viewed rather strictly as men's work or women's; a "good" wife was presumed to do her women's work in her realm, the home. Until recently it was taken for granted that the wife's lesser development and "nonworking" (meaning not working outside the home for pay) status were compatible with and conducive to companionship.

But can a marriage of two unequal people blossom into a companionate relationship, especially if they start out relatively equal and then through performing their sexually determined roles in family life gradually become unequal? Doesn't companionate marriage presuppose a union of equals? A basic requirement for justice is that one person not obtain fuller opportunities for human development at the expense of another. Isn't this a key argument for partnership marriage? On the positive side, only a relationship of equality will satisfy our human yearning for community.

Milton wrote, "It is not the joining of another body that will remove loneliness, but the uniting of another compliable mind." Such a meeting of minds can come only between equals, true partners.

Still, even though equality may be a necessity for all adults in a family, is it more of a threat than a hope? It depends on whom you're asking! We would all agree that companionship and equality are a challenge to rigid sex roles in the family and society. This is a real threat, both to the nuclear family and to society *as they are.* It requires change, in people and in structures. That requires adjustment and involves stress, tension, and conflict, in individuals and between people, especially married couples. It also may involve exhilaration and a sense of liberation, accompanied by a flowering of creativity and new life in individuals and relationships. Change and conflict are inevitable, but change and even conflict may lead to growth and relational vitality.

AUTONOMY WITHIN INTIMACY

The family with two or more adults is a partnership of autonomous individuals covenanted together in some type of intimate relationship. This means that the identity and selfhood of each is valued and developed, enriched, *within* the family and *because* of the quality of the relationship. The intimacy is enhanced because of the interest each has in the uniqueness of the other or others. This is autonomy within intimacy.

Full intimacy cannot be realized with someone who is an image rather than a real flesh-and-blood person. We must be who we are and reveal this real self to our partner, and this partner must be open and accepting of our unique selfhood, and vice versa, in order for an intimate relationship to develop and grow. We can't claim to love without this kind of knowledge and appreciation of our partner. What is required is a just love, a love that corresponds to the reality of the one loved. Thus, justice requires that each affirm for the other what that one truly needs in order to live as a full human person. Any pattern of relationship that doesn't respect the partner in these needs and claims is an unjust pattern of relationship. The love necessary for an intimate relationship is a just love. The family involves a covenant of mutuality, of mutual possibilities for full human development for all.

In conventional nuclear marriage the husband's full development and whole personhood haven't been in question; the wife's selfhood has. Indeed, women have literally been dependent, economically and psychologically, on their husbands, and our culture has approved and promoted this childlikeness as "feminine." Husbands grew through work and contacts in their realm, "man's world," whereas women often supported their husbands' growth at the expense of their own. What is needed is love of partners toward each other as whole, valued human beings, in integrated autonomy and intimacy.

SOME ELEMENTS OF FAMILY COVENANT

The goal of family life might be expressed as shalom: peace, wholeness, well-being, union, health, growth in personhood and in caring, becoming partners—of each other in the family and of the family toward the world.

Some elements that Wilson Yates recommends in "The Family: A New Pluralism and a New Wholeness" for a covenantal understanding of the family are:

- Commitment of persons to the creation of a life of intimate companionship in the full span of their relations with each other
- Commitment to create a fabric of honesty, trust, openness, and acceptance
- Commitment to explore the religious and moral depths of human existence
- Creation of boundaries that define the major patterns of behavior in the family (negotiation and renegotiation of the rules the family lives by)
- Commitment to an ethic of wholeness that will give direction for the adults' actions toward each

other, other family members, and the world and will lead to responsibility for the well-being of each partner, any children in the family, and the larger society; an ethic focusing on love, justice, and freedom

CARING

The family cannot be treated as an isolated unit that can thrive and sustain itself without broader nurturing and challenging networks of relationship. Interpersonal love between two or more persons doesn't and shouldn't exist in isolation. The family exists in community, and ideally the love of that family is enhanced by and contributes to that community. Just as we love because God first loved us, so we love and do justice in community because we experience love in our families. The experience of love ensues in a response of love beyond ourselves. Beverly and James Harrison's definition of marriage includes the expectation of growth "in the capacity for caring (not merely caring for each other, but caring)." This is a *relational* ethic for marriage in which family love is held to be a *moral* relation (not just a status) expected to contribute to mutual love of the partners and enrichment of their relationship, personal growth of each member, and love for others. From this ethical perspective, we can claim that the interpersonal love and self-actualization realized in a good family relationship should also result in loving action for the upbuilding of our sisters and brothers in society, especially those most vulnerable, and of social institutions that mediate justice in society.

MONEY AND FINANCE

The family's standard of living and how the family gets and spends its income are worthy of attention. They involve:

- Crucial decisions about work
- Time and effort spent doing the work
- Life-style and stewardship values related to consumption, investing, saving, and giving
- Decisions about *how* money and work decisions are to be made
- Management of money
- Stress and tension from inadequate income, unemployment, workplace tensions, job changes, and conflicts of values related to any of these

Working for pay is a means for life—"earning a *living*"—and often becomes involved in family conflict. It looms so large in importance for individual families and our society that it requires thoughtful attention.

EARNING A LIVING

There are several ways that earning a living affects families. Especially in marriage, the adults may decide *who* is going to work and *when* in their life cycle, related to decisions about having children and child care:

Will both partners work outside the home?

Will one (usually the wife) work until they have children and then resume work after the children are in school or grown?

Can they live on the income thus earned?

What kind of child care will they try to get if both work regularly?

How do they both *feel* about their decisions about work?

Some couples consider such alternatives as shared jobs (thus they can share child care, but they earn only one salary) or employment for the wife with house care for the husband. Some couples even choose the kind of work they will do and the hours they'll do it in accord with life-style values. Most couples these days meet, however, when they already have jobs or are studying for particular professions, or they get married and take whatever one or both can find for employment in order to survive. Mostly, our *jobs* determine our time and affect our families; seldom can people mold their work life to fit their home life.

Jobs affect families. The kind of work done affects the kinds of persons the members become; their tension level; time available together (one may travel to work, or they may work different shifts, or an executive works late, or they may have a weekend marriage because of someone's work in a different town); time available for children, housekeeping, and recreation; and certainly their satisfaction in life. And work determines the amount of family income available, except for those families receiving unemployment or welfare benefits and the tiny minority who receive money from investment income in addition to or instead of paid jobs. Adult family members may have little choice about what kind of work they'll do or how much it pays; they sometimes must take what's available and then work out a way to live on what they're paid.

Work patterns may change (by choice or circumstance). Often we women have gone back to or begun work outside the home after our children are older. Sometimes a husband's mid-life crisis results in a radical change of kind and place of work, perhaps because of renewed value placed on his family and a humane life-style. And, of course, both retirement and unemployment greatly affect families.

SPENDING AND MANAGING MONEY

Insufficient income is a major cause of family unhappiness and conflict. And so is the spending and managing of income. Both family and cultural background and values influence the way we feel about money and the experience we have in managing it. Two people may not know this about each other until they begin living together, unless counseling has brought differences to light in structured discussion and planning about money.

Planning money management and budgeting is an important task of families, in order to live on the available income and avoid the conflicts that arise when money runs out before the next paycheck, and in order to work out cooperatively the best use of money, including saving for future use such as vacations, a house, and children's education. Partners have to decide whether to have a joint bank account and pool their resources or keep their money separate (at least some of it), with possibly each paying for certain family expenses. They have to work out how to *decide* what purchases to make, how much to pledge to the church, how much to spend for relatives' Christmas gifts or for one partner's clothing and the other's bowling. And they have to agree on *who* will pay the bills, balance the checkbook, and do the income tax—and *when*. Married couples sometimes decide this on the basis of sex roles (the husband takes care of money matters, because "men earn the money and understand math"), but sometimes it's on the basis of who has the time or the interest.

Spending, saving, and handling money may be unifying or divisive aspects of a family.

Leah and Ralph, both strongly committed to the church, became tithers as soon as they were married—a mutual decision to act out their faith in this concrete way and to establish their marriage on this foundation. They also feel unity and gratification in contributing to organizations doing work for justice that they care about deeply.

Earl and Mickie had always been "one" with their money and never had any serious financial worries. But when Mickie's brother borrowed money from them and delayed repaying it for many months, they argued for the first time over what's mine and what's yours—money *and* relatives.

Dealing with money matters is a prime case for the need for open and intentional communication. It also requires not just goodwill but planning and discipline. But for many families, all this cannot outweigh the influence of the economic system on their chances of getting work at all and on their level of income. Adult family members may simply have to work two jobs—if they can find them—and forget the luxury of considering the effect on their relationship of excessive fatigue and inadequate time together; economic survival is the priority, and the family doesn't call the shots; the external economic system does. Thus, a lot about money that greatly affects families is beyond the partners' range of decision. Yet, society—and even the church sometimes—blames a couple, not inflation or the unemployment rate, when a marriage doesn't survive the pressure of economic stress.

BREAKDOWN AND ENRICHMENT
OF FAMILY LIFE

BREAKDOWN

Reasons for marital dissatisfaction, divorce, and dissolution of various other kinds of families are more numerous than those given at the time of legal divorce in court. They include:

mental cruelty	sexual incompatibility
neglect	in-laws, relatives
physical abuse	excessive demands
financial problems	differing values
drinking	nonsupport
infidelity	husband dominant
verbal abuse	unsatisfactory home
lack of love	life
desertion	

Other factors in the partners' backgrounds or circumstances contribute to separations or are related to high divorce rates:

urban dwelling (current or childhood)	nonattendance at church
husband's low income	low parental income
large number of siblings	childlessness
parental divorce	early pregnancy
either spouse previously divorced	elopement
teenage marriage	lack of supportive relationships with friends and family

Sidney Jourard observes that marriages rarely fail; rather, *people* fail *marriages*. Some reasons:

- a lack of give-and-take
- a lack of concern or respect for a partner's need to become more self-sufficient emotionally or otherwise
- a lack of toleration for differences of opinions
- a lack of sex-role flexibility
- a tendency to cherish our mates as "they used to be"
- a lack of both empathy and understanding during life's trying moments
- a lack of a sense of humor (a must for the preservation of sanity of any marriage)
- a tendency to take love for granted
- a growing inability to share either joy or pain

Family estrangement is a process. Divorce doesn't come out of the blue, though the first year or so of marriage is a particularly crucial period, with many divorces occurring then. If the couple weathers that first year and the birth of the first child, the divorce rate diminishes slowly with increasing years of marriage. Conflict, as we have pointed out before, does not necessarily mean a bad or unhappy marriage or other family relationship. It may well be a sign of health and the occasion for growth and change that will strengthen the relationship. In fact, the near-total absence of conflict is clearly one sign of a devitalized marriage: there may be little intense emotion of any kind (humor, zest) expressed in such a marriage, as well as low expectations for its outcome. It may also be a sign of emotional suppression, perhaps to keep up the facade of what the couple thinks is a good marriage or what they think society or their relatives expect of marriage; or one may suppress hostility and conflict out of fear of losing—or becoming revealed to—the other; in these cases they are playing a role. Realistic conflict can be a means of open-

ing up a family relationship to change, leading to clari-
fication in individual and mutual goals, accommodation
of differences, or reconsideration of family roles. Constructive conflict is "complaining without blaming,"
writes Gail Fullerton. It must follow rules of playing fair
and not going too far, listening to the complaint and being intentional about the way the complaint is made, not
bringing up a whole laundry list of old grievances that
no longer matter. Conflict involving legitimate com-
plaints can be resolved through humor, persuasion, and
negotiation or through arbitration by a family counselor.

But other family conflicts are not constructive. Some
quarrels over one issue are really a symptom of a more
deep-seated dissatisfaction. Some occur simply to vent
steam, to release tension or frustration from some other
cause. Strained relations and growing hostility may
build up, becoming a pattern of family life. Certain code
words or gestures become flash points, used viciously to
trigger an expected response. The conflict escalates.

On the other hand, the meaninglessness and boredom
of some family life may drag on and on, largely unnoticed but draining.

Marriage and other family relationships do not fail at
one clearly identifiable point, but there may come, at
some particular moment, the *recognition* that the relationship is wrong, the conflict—or the beating—unbear-
able; surely there must be more to life than this. An
extramarital affair may cause or result from such recognition. Or perhaps further withdrawal from the partner
will occur. There may be ups and downs in the process
of estrangement, one fearing the loss of the other or the
stress or scandal of a failed relationship. But at some
point, discussion of divorce becomes a decision to act, or
the partners decide to separate, or one family member
leaves. The family unit has broken down and may or
may not be reconciled.

ENRICHMENT

Christian ethics of the family and marriage should be concerned less with maintenance of the status of marriage and more with the well-being of the persons in the relationship. Often, however, the church has been indifferent to or avoided the needs of Christian families, including marriage, while, of course, sanctifying marriage with ceremony and lip service. Fortunately, there are new approaches to evangelism directed toward commitment to be a truly Christian family, reflective of Jesus' declaration to Zacchaeus, "This day is salvation come to this house" (Luke 19:19, KJV). Family ministry programs of some churches focus on marriage, on prevention of marital problems, and on the dynamic. Model church programs include couple evangelism, marriage enrichment retreats, marriage support system, and service and outreach.

Marriage enrichment is a focus fairly recently taken up by most denominations. It is an ecumenical movement, with many programs and retreats, including couples from several denominations. It emphasizes self-knowledge, knowledge of spouse, spiritual development, and communication. There is a national Association of Couples for Marriage Enrichment. For many it has brought new depth and vitality into marriage, contributed an approach to conflict resolution, and provided a support group; they are evangelists, proclaiming this good news about newly found potential in marriage.

Marriage enrichment contributes both to the well-being of the persons who are married and to the support of marriage by church and society. It assumes that persons created in God's image have the right, responsibility, and potentiality to grow and develop their full personhood. One writer on middle-aged marriage says that marriage enrichment for the middle-aged couple should not focus on improving the marriage so much as on improving the human beings in it; it can be an antidote to middle-age character deterioration! As we've seen before, vital people make vital relationships, and middle age may be a good time to renew our quest for personal identity and mission in life. Women's search for identity and for full personhood, a major focus of the feminist movement, may also be part of marriage enrichment, strengthening us for equality in both marriage and the rest of life. This may upset the status quo and bring conflict, but growth can surely result from personal development and thereby strengthen both persons and marriage. This is not, however, an area of universal church commitment. In fact, as we've already noted, some see it as a threat to Christian faith and Christian marriage.

Church concern for the well-being of the persons in marriage should also focus literally on their physical well-being. Marriage ethics should bring to light physical abuse in marriage and the family: the battering of wives and children (and a few husbands) and elderly relatives, rape in marriage, and incest. And the church should address hard ethical questions about whether the traditional structure of marriage serves the well-being of women.

The church can also enrich marriage through developing support programs. Primary examples are the marriage enrichment programs and retreats themselves. Couples attending become a support group for one another's marriages and for marriage in general in their various churches. People *talk* about marriage, its joys and its problems; they talk about discoveries and good ways to approach certain matters in marriage. Marriage doesn't remain isolated in the private realm. Support also includes prophetic preaching on and study of some of the primary social factors that have a negative impact on marriage, advocacy for changing these conditions, and short-term remedial help for couples suffering under some of these conditions.

CHAPTER 3

Social Witness of the Family

Just as the self is not isolated but rather a social being developing personhood in relationships with other human beings, especially the family, so the family is not an isolated, self-sufficient entity but rather one social institution among many that make up society. We have seen that the ways in which the family interrelates with other social institutions significantly affect the performance of its functions—in some ways positively and in other ways negatively. In most cases society affects the family; some examples are the socialization of children by the mass media; the "weekend marriage" life-style, determined by location and availability of work or family breakup related to unemployment and the structure of welfare system; and the powerful cultural influence on sex roles within the family. The social context of families is oppressive of racial minority groups, poor people, and women and is full of both fear and apathy. Some families suffer this firsthand, while others, in family castles, are protected from it and therefore isolated from both victims and those working for change.

But the family also acts within society, taking the initiative on behalf of its own members or other individuals or groups in society. Many of us have brought about change—small or large—in another part of society. Examples are:

- Interceding for a child in the school system who has been tracked in a slow-learners group by virtue of being black or Hispanic or having a handicap unrelated to learning ability
- Advocating the inclusion of black literature and observance of Black History Month in our child's school
- Advocating day care in the workplace where one of the family is employed
- Refusing, along with others, to buy some product whose manufacturer is involved in social injustice, and succeeding either in getting the boycotted product withdrawn from a local market or in changing the unjust condition

Whole families are now participating in demonstrations against nuclear weapons in advocacy of their own and humanity's survival.

Often, however, families feel relatively helpless or apathetic in the face of the vastness, complexity, and power of the surrounding social system. When they turn to each other, in small community organizations or the church, and experience the support and energy of like-minded folk and the strength that comes from finding that a conviction is shared by others, they are encouraged to take the initiative rather than accept their dependency in society. Within the caring community of the family, individuals develop sensitivity to themselves, other family members, and society. Thus personal fulfillment, justice, and service are not opposites but interrelated possibilities and together contribute to the upbuilding of persons, of community among the close groups of family and church, and of a just society.

ACTION WITHIN THE CHURCH

Families seeking to develop such ethical maturity may find within the church at its best not only the inspiration and imperative for doing so but also the means. The church is a worldwide inclusive community crosscutting national boundaries, races, and classes and bringing families at the grass roots into potentially intimate contact both with the richness of other cultures and with human suffering among families in other parts of the world.

DEVELOPING AWARENESS

Within the body of Christ, ethically sensitive families may develop awareness of the human condition and human richness. Some ways to broaden the family's perspective of the world and its people include:

- Sharing music and prayers about and from the world church, such as the *Worship Book* of the World Council of Churches' Assembly, which contains marvelous music and worship resources from many Christian traditions, and the WCC's *Ecumenical Prayer Cycle*, with information and prayers from churches all over the world
- Praying for the known needy close at hand and those reported in the daily news
- Observing UN Day, Human Rights Day, and UNICEF in the church and in family Halloween custom
- Celebrating World Day of Prayer and Week of Christian Unity in church and family and, especially, ecumenically in the community
- Participating in church conferences and camps and visiting other churches (especially ethnic or

racial churches different from your own or churches of other Christian traditions)

• Choosing pen pals among children or families from other countries and even in a different language from your own

• Being a host family for an international student or family

• Participating in an international student exchange for a summer or year

• Holding church suppers and intergenerational educational programs about life and issues of justice in other parts of the world

• Traveling and living in other countries as a family

• Reading pastoral letters from overseas Christian bodies that communicate the anguish of injustice, war, or poverty they are experiencing in their countries

• Reading statements of concern on current issues of world peace and justice from denominational offices and the National Council of Churches

WITNESSING FOR PEACE AND JUSTICE

With such heightened awareness and sustained study of chosen areas, families may join together in action committed to making a witness for justice and peace and contributing in at least some small concrete way to substantive change. Family social action may include everything from family letters to Congress opposing budgetary appropriations for new weapons systems or military intervention in some country the family has lived in, to demonstrations protesting against those same issues or to cooperative renovation of a house with other families in your neighborhood for low-income housing or elderly group living. There may be several such family social-action task forces in your church, and they could share their experience and reflection regularly with the congregation in the educational curriculum, worship services, Bible studies, and so on, and be further strengthened by ongoing congregational study and reflection on underlying or parallel issues in other parts of the world or in scripture.

INVOLVING THE WHOLE FAMILY

In their fine book *Parenting for Peace and Justice,* Kathleen and James McGinnis list six principles for family involvement in social action:

1. Regularly inviting children to join parents in social action
2. Seeking broad exposure to advocates, victims, and situations
3. Inviting children to actions within their capabilities
4. Trying to integrate fun whenever possible
5. Choosing involvement that is "doing with" rather than "doing for"
6. Assuming social-action involvement in the works of justice as well as the works of mercy

They conclude with a statement of their conviction that prayer and social action must be integrated. We need to experience social action as part of the very substance of our faith, they say, and to know that Jesus walks with us. Prayer unites us with the whole body of Christ and deepens family unity at the same time. In the McGinnises' experience (p. 3),

> social ministry and family ministry enrich each other. That is, the more community, the more we are building our family community. And vice versa, we are coming to see that part of our social minis-

try as a family is to build our family community. In-
tegrating the "apostolic life," the "family life," and
the so-called "spiritual life" keeps us from the
schizophrenia that sunders the wholeness of Christian living—the full Gospel.

For many families, the social ministry of building family community could well involve combatting the negative social forces that work against the family, such as
racism, unemployment, wide wage disparities, and sexism. If we eliminate the last, though the family will
change, it will surely be stronger for being more just and
equal. Certainly, a necessary social ministry for the family is addressing and acting against family violence and
sexual abuse. And social action against discrimination
because of sexual orientation would contribute to the
healing of breaches within families of gay and lesbian
persons, and to their establishing viable family units.
These are all social ministries focusing more or less directly on the family itself. The Family Cluster Movement (see Margaret M. Sawin, ed., *Hope for Families*) is
a sound and creative vehicle for directly strengthening
the family and intentionally building community within
the family by way of regular intergenerational gather-
ings of several other similar families for programmed activity and mutual support.

ACTION IN THE WORLD

There are other forms of social ministry, in which the
family goes into the world in mission for justice, for the
sake of others; these ministries, too, enrich the family.
God's empowering love is replenished by being shared.
In this day of grave concern about the family as a viable
institution, we may be able to strengthen the family best
by devoting ourselves as families to imperatives beyond

ourselves. Such social ministries attend to the cries of other families near and far: migrant workers who suffer from low pay, seasonal employment, and inadequate schooling and health care for their children; homeless families in our cities who had houses and jobs only months ago; refugee families fleeing for their lives from political and military repression; landless families whose islands have been irradiated or obliterated by nuclear testing; fearless mothers whose children have "disappeared" and who, when they protest, disappear as well; families whose daughters are forced into prostitution for tourism; destitute families of women, children, and the old, living in segregated "homelands," whose men work in South African cities all year separated from their families; and families in the Soviet Union, Holland, Canada, the United States, Japan, and elsewhere around the globe who live in deep fear of nuclear annihilation. Truly attending to these realities of other human families around the world forcibly drives into our consciousness the realization that the world is not as it should be and that we are called to act for change. As families we can engage in such committed social action.

God's will for the human race is that the relations among all people should be a covenant relationship, like that of a family. The Christian symbol for this relationship is the shared meal of the Lord's Supper, the eucharist; and what is more familiar or more central to the family than a shared meal? The Lord's Supper symbolizes God's covenant with us, as the family of God; and as we eat at table together, so we go out in eucharistic action to the world, sharing food with the hungry and enabling justice for the oppressed. God's covenant is both a moral *imperative*, to act in neighborly concern for the whole world, and *grace*, a gift that makes response to the imperative possible.

The family, then, is sociologically part of the wider social system, interrelated with other institutions that make up society and theologically part of the family of God, gathering at the Lord's Table and going out in eucharistic mission of charity and justice. We are, willy-nilly, part of society, often buffeted by social forces that sorely stress the family. To participate in society intentionally, as families committed to transformation toward the realization of shalom in community, is to hearten and give strength and hope to families everywhere. With the company of believers, families may build caring community in which individual persons are affirmed as "subjects of their lives" with gifts for ministry; close, supportive community is celebrated and nurtured, and, with renewed strength for individual and corporate ministry, social ministry to the pain and injustice of the structures of global society is carried out.

PART II

Women
in Family Life

CHAPTER 4

Becoming a Woman-Self in the Family

The women we are as adults reflect the experiences we had as children, learning what being female involves. This chapter considers the elements of our upbringing that strongly affect our identity as women and the roles we recognize as appropriate.

FAMILY INFLUENCES ON IDENTITY

The family is of particular significance in identity. Identity is developed within the family, and individuals are identified as members of specific families. ("She's one of the Bellinghams," someone says, defining an individual at least partly in terms of this basic social unit, which forms her and through which she encounters other institutions and people in the society.) The family is the first community in which human sociality is developed and nurtured; the family is the social context in which the individual becomes a person, a social being. We develop our identity as particular social beings, with unique personalities, first of all through our relationships in the family: with parents, perhaps with siblings, and possibly with other persons in the home such as extended family members. And these relationships are affected by such things as our position in the family (middle child, only child, baby), our gender, and the age of our parents.

PARENTS

The most influential relationship is the one with our parents. Haven't you often found yourself doing or saying something just like your mother and, when you stop to think about it, realizing that there's no real reason to have done or said it this way except that your mother would have? We internalize our mothers and fathers and become like them in many ways. Yet we also resist this as part of maturing, developing a distinct identity and autonomy from our parents—and sometimes consciously developing an identity as opposite to them as possible. Yet either way we carry a conflict as we continue to recognize a parent in our own selfhood. The same thing occurs with our own children: Sometimes the thing we most dislike in one child is a characteristic we recognize in ourself.

RACE AND CLASS

Within the family we are socialized into our own selfhood and into a culture and world view. Here the influence of race and social class contributes much to our identity. The larger culture of race, class, and possibly ethnicity is transmitted through the family to the individual, and the individual is formed partly by these influences. Thus we are different people from what we would have been in another family, with different parents, with or without siblings, richer or poorer, born of a different race or nationality, born or adopted into a different position in the family—and certainly different from what we would be had we been male instead of female.

Yet the human being is also amazingly resilient, and

personal identity is unique and strong. Very different persons grow up in the same family, strong individuals emerge from very difficult family and cultural situations, and people with problems emerge from strong and loving families. Our identity is strongly affected by our social environment, especially family, yet there is also the potential to be unique individuals, autonomous selves.

GROWING UP FEMALE

Another aspect of identity and the family is related to growing up. In our family relationships this is sometimes not adequately taken into account, not in adolescence and perhaps not even in adulthood. Identity develops through stages of childhood into adolescence, when the search for identity becomes an important tool. Rebelling against parents and family values is part of the process of seeking identity as an autonomous individual. Sometimes adopted children become particularly interested in their biological parents at this point, as part of a search for their own identity. Family relationships shift in accord with developing identity: "Mom, I'm *fifteen* years old, you know!" Sometimes they don't shift enough in adulthood: At work and in relationships with friends or spouse and children, we may relate as adults but may still be treated as children by our parents; we may even revert to dependent behavior with them. Our adult identity is thus insecure. Lastly, women may shift from a dependent relationship with parents to dependence on husbands, failing to develop their identity as real adults. This is due especially to sex roles, which are a strong influence on identity in our culture.

GENDER

Gender is an especially significant aspect of identity. Girls and boys have different experiences of gender identity formation. For daughters, identity is developed in terms of being like their mothers and being attached to them (as the primary caretakers); while for sons, identity means being different from the caretaker mother and becoming unattached. Therefore, females develop a sense of self as less separate from the rest of the world, more related to others and the world, than males do. The self becomes defined as relational, women develop identity as beings-in-relationship, and relationship is associated with caring. (However, our society values autonomy and rugged individualism much more highly than being in relationship.)

Gender identification is established by about age three: girls and boys recognize the appropriate behavior and personality characteristics for boys and girls and know that it is more advantageous to be male.

SEX ROLES

There is an important distinction between gender (female or male) and sex role (feminine or masculine). Gender is indicated by physical distinctions, most simply by distinctive genitals. But sex roles are dichotomized roles for females and males based on presumed innate differences between the two genders. A sex role is a set of behavioral, temperamental, emotional, intellectual, and attitudinal characteristics identified, in a given culture at a given time, as feminine or masculine. Characteristics of maleness and femaleness are generally not biologically determined but are based on cultural definitions of sex-appropriate behavior; cultural learning greatly influences distinctive sex roles.

GROWING UP IN FAMILY AND SOCIETY

The process by which people learn and internalize or integrate cultural definitions of sex-appropriate behavior is part of the overall process of socialization. Girls and boys learn sex roles through a process of socialization that begins and is especially strong and significant in our families in our earliest years and continues throughout our lives. This socialization process is reinforced by various institutions of society. Children learn female and male sex roles from direct teaching, absorption of cultural values, observation of actual sex-role differentiation in their families and surrounding society (and in the wider society through the mass media), and from social control mechanisms in different institutions. An easy translation is made from "what *is*" to "what's *natural*" to "what's *right*."

PARENTS

Parents surely play the major role in the general socialization process and in specific sex-role identity and behavior. Infant daughters are held, touched, and talked to more than infant sons and are handled more gently. Studies show that parents try to promote very different characteristics, abilities, and skills in girls and boys, according to traditional ideas of masculinity and femininity. This includes different toys, social characteristics, and books as well as explicit teaching about the relative worth of the two sexes. By school age, children learn to distinguish between females and males and recognize characteristic behaviors of each, express appropriate sex-role preferences for themselves, and behave in accord with sex-role standards. Children observe in their families and society that females and males do different things and that males have more power, prestige, and freedom. Some studies show that, by six, most boys see males as more powerful, aggressive, authoritative, and smarter than females, and most girls agree with them. Girls prefer the male role more than boys prefer the female role, yet they have also internalized their own sex role as right for them.

There are, however, notable differences in sex-role socialization of children in some families. In most cases of women who have pursued "deviant" options in adulthood (such as having careers without marrying, or not having children, or putting their families second), their most positive socialization came from their fathers, who encouraged these daughters (perhaps an only child) to enter a "masculine" field and pursue a career. Such women have also had supportive husbands or had mothers who were models for successfully combining working (perhaps in a male-dominated field) with family life.

There are racial and class differences from this general socialization process. Black families tend to have either no significant difference in aspirations for sons and daughters or even higher educational aspirations for their daughters than sons, and working is regarded as an appropriate female role in most black families. Further, black parents generally restrict their daughters' freedom of activity less than do white parents. Finally, working-class parents may pressure their daughters toward the traditional female role even more than do middle-class parents.

RESTRICTIONS OF SEX ROLES

Through sex roles, women's personhood has been restricted. Invariably, the characteristics and functions assigned to women have been designated through the years as inferior, less healthy, and less valuable in society than those assigned to men, and women have been denied access to most spheres of society except the home. Sex roles may be summarized as "women can't do" and "men must do."

It is oppressive to be dependent, without an identity of one's own. Neither child raising nor housework is a full-time occupation throughout a woman's lifetime. Women are now having fewer children, and they have more than thirty-five years after the last child enters school to do something other than full-time child care. In addition, of course, many women do not marry or do not have children. Nor is the role of consumer or sex symbol usually a satisfactory substitute for full use of a woman's talents and energies. To be denied opportunity for work, creativity, learning, and service on the basis of gender is oppressive.

But the seduction of the inferior role should not be overlooked either, and it too has a negative effect: the role provides exemption from decision making, a life of luxury and leisure for upper-class women, informal power (woman behind the man), ability to change social class through marriage, and ascribed status without the necessity of earning status, prestige, or esteem. Indeed, laziness may be one cost of the inferior sex role for some women who can afford it, a cost that seduces some women into resisting liberation.

We women especially need to become autonomous human beings, with separate and distinct personalities, while still maintaining our relationality. We need to become the *subjects* of our lives, self-initiating and defining actors, not objects of life, acted upon or derivative beings. We are human persons and therefore entitled to free development of full personhood: individuality, strengths and weaknesses, talents, preferences, and human rights, as well as human responsibilities.

FULL PERSONHOOD

Should a Christian woman ever put herself first? Is this what self-realization really means? Does Christian love require the sacrifice of whole personhood, of personal identity as a whole human being, the sacrifice of a fully rounded life for the sake of our families, for the good of society, and even for the sake of our femininity, our womanhood?

Personal actualization is not individualistic or selfish, a me-only concern. To ask women to deny themselves for others wrongs both women *and* the Christian concept of love; it is a selfish and narrow view of Christian love and the Christian family and a form of suicide for women. The individual good of a woman should not be sacrificed to a supposed social good when what is at stake is the fundamental dignity of the individual. This is unjust love, which denies the reality of women.

Women are of infinite worth, created in the image of God. Christian love does not require self-denial to the point of sacrifice of identity. In fact it requires—and empowers—full development of personhood and self-acceptance. We are created in God's image and are called to be good stewards of God's creation. We are redeemed by Christ's act on the cross and are empowered to love ourselves and others by our experience of God's love. We have been given gifts for ministry—talents—and are called to be good and faithful stewards of these gifts. To restrict half of God's children in our exercise of these gifts is a denial of God and a rejection of the abundant life that Christ gives as part of the new creation. We are all, the whole People of God, called to ministry. We can respond only as whole, self-affirming persons.

Pride is not women's characteristic sin; women's sin is more nearly self-abnegation. Man's sin is that he has not had enough humility and rather has usurped power and dominated all; woman's sin is too much humility, failure to acknowledge her God-given selfhood with a full range of human characteristics and her gifts for ministry. Human growth into the rich potential created by God cannot be contrary to God's will. Surely it is a Christian duty for women, as it is for other oppressed "nonpersons," to struggle for personal worth and recognition of the image of God in ourselves and, within the Christian community, to seek to identify our individual gifts for ministry. This is what is meant by the ministry of the laity.

CHAPTER 5

Self and Marriage

When you think of marriage, what do you see in your mind? Where did you get your vision of marriage? In your mental image of marriage, what is the range of married experiences you think of? The length of time pictured? How many people are in your image of marriage? What is the relation of marriage to the wider society in your mind's eye? Is the church in your picture? In what role? Does your idea of marriage agree or conflict with the general ideal of marriage most people seem to have? With your parents' marriage? With your own real experience, either of your own marriage or of all the other marriages you know?

These are questions about what we think marriage *is*. In addition, there are questions about happiness or satisfaction—or even survival—in marriage. Do you think society as a whole has a positive view of marriage? Do you? Do your friends? Are women's perceptions of marriage different from men's? Many more married men than married women report that they are satisfied in marriage. Is marriage different for women and men? Have we entered marriage with different images of what it is, with different expectations, with different needs?

CHANGES IN MARRIAGE TODAY

There have been significant changes in marriage over the past two decades.

- It is no longer assumed as the life-style for all
- It is often postponed
- Couples live together without marriage in increasing numbers
- Marriage patterns have changed, especially in sex-role division of labor
- Many more married women with children are working outside the home, earning a share of the family income
- Choice is being exercised about children
- Sexual exclusivity is no longer taken for granted by all couples as the definition for marital fidelity

WHY CHOOSE MARRIAGE?

When I was a young woman, finishing college and working in the fifties in the South, marriage-and-children before thirty was a social expectation for all white southern women. It was not a question of *if*, or even *when* (you were expected to marry immediately after college, certainly to find your mate during college or as soon as you started working); the only question was *who*. This expectation exerted a powerful influence and continued to do so for the next twenty years.

One of the striking changes today is that marriage has become much more a matter of choice, of decision. Women are considering whether or not to marry, and when, as well as who they might want to marry. What considerations do we bring to these decisions? We understand philosophically and theologically, and from our own experience when we think about it, that humans are social beings by nature; we are relational creatures, destined by our Creator for communion, with each other and with God. We know that we do not develop as humans without human contact; we need each other. Love is a primary example of human communion, and the marriage of a woman and a man is the traditional way such love is expressed, though by no means the only way.

Why do women choose marriage?

SEARCH FOR SUPPORTIVE INTIMACY

We really do long for deep, intimate communion with a special other, communion in which we can share ourself as we really are and be received, supported, and nurtured; a communion in which we can thrive and grow and be at peace. Women especially are raised as relational beings, so it is not surprising that we might choose marriage for relational reasons. (The reality of marriage may not, however, meet our hopes and expectations.)

ECONOMIC SURVIVAL

For many women, economic survival is a compelling reason for marriage. It is difficult for women to be completely self-supporting in the U.S. economy, with its underemployment and underpaid employment for women and its other examples of institutionalized sexism. And for a great many women in our society economic necessity is still a powerful reason for staying in a marriage.

SEXUAL RELATIONSHIP

Though marriage is not necessary for sexual relationship, many of us wish to engage in sexual relations within marriage for religious and social reasons. For many the permanence and security of marriage enhances and frees sexual expression.

DESIRE FOR CHILDREN
The desire for children and a partnership in which to raise and nurture them is obviously a strong motivation for marriage.

PERSONAL GROWTH
The opportunity for personal growth within the context of the social relationship of marriage is also sometimes recognized and valued by women.

WHAT IS MARRIAGE?

What do we understand marriage to be? What kind of a relationship is it?

MARRIAGE AS COVENANT
In religious terms, marriage may be understood as a covenant, an agreement made by two people before God and in the presence of the community of believers and witnesses. We get our idea of covenant from the story in the Bible of God making a covenant with Abraham and Sarah and thereby with the people of Israel: God would be their God and they would be God's people. This was a promise and established a structured, specialized relationship.

We also get our idea of marriage covenant partly from the biblical comparison of the covenant relationship between Christ and the church to the relationship between husband and wife. But this model has implied a hierarchical relationship of dominance of one member (Christ or husband) and submission of the other (church or wife). Such a model for marriage, in which husbands are in the place of Christ and thereby would, by implication, receive the worship and service of wives who are in the place of the church, is, of course, idolatrous. It is also bad for marriage, a relationship between human beings who are *only* human but equally made in God's image, and it is incompatible with intimacy, which is the core of marriage.

God's love as promised in the covenants and revealed in Jesus Christ is the norm for our relationships in marriage. Relationships that center in and bring forth wholeness, caring, openness, and dignity between partners affirm God's covenant, in marriage and in other human relationships such as the church. The gospel message speaks to life's crucial questions of who we are, how we relate to one another, and how we respond to the love of God. The covenant of marriage engages these questions in light of the gospel proclamation of the good news of God's love.

MARRIAGE "CONTRACTS"

Contract is different from covenant; it is a legal term and relationship. A contract is really about *limits* of a relationship between *separate* parties; only so much is involved between the parties. Covenant is an agreement to enter into relationship that involves shared life together—to become "we." (God said, "I . . . will be your God, and you shall be my people" [Lev. 26:12].) It is about the shared life, the openness and commitment to the other, not about the limits. Of course, in marriage there *are* limits; we do not literally become one, submerged in each other's identity. And nowadays some people speak of working out marriage contracts, spelling out some new understandings of egalitarian marriage. I think this is, in most cases, still included within the meaning of covenant (and might be better expressed without use of a legal term). This same understanding might be reached in premarital counseling. Couples need to talk intentionally about what they expect in marriage. Working out a marriage "contract" may simply be a systematic way of doing this. (Of course, it might also be a contract in the literal sense, focusing on the limits of the agreement rather than a commitment to a "we partnership.")

MARITAL RELATIONSHIPS
IN CONTEMPORARY FAMILY

There is, as we all recognize in the lives of our friends, quite a variety of marital relationships—couples' ways of sharing a home, rearing children, expressing sexuality, living in the outside world, and so on. One way of looking at these relationships is in terms of sex roles and the relative equality of the spouses in the marriage.

TRADITIONAL MARRIAGE

In a traditional or patriarchal marriage the husband is dominant and independent while the wife is subordinate or submissive and dependent on him economically and psychologically. He is the financial provider and she the nurturer of relationships. His realm is the outside world and hers the home. Each performs rather clear gender-related roles. The family pattern is hierarchical, with the husband-father at the top of the pyramid, looked up to and depended on by the rest of the family and making major decisions, though the wife-mother is far more active in the daily affairs of the home, especially with the children. The family is the primary focus of her life, while it is only part of his life; in their relationship she may give all of herself and he only a part. He may relate to her in a somewhat fatherly manner, and she may try to be a girlfriend to him.

CO-EQUAL MARRIAGE

Here the traditional pattern is modified toward greater equality for the wife and more of a part for her in the traditional masculine roles, while the husband helps with household tasks and child care. They might divide responsibility and authority for different areas, recognizing the abilities and interests of each. She may be more independent, perhaps working outside the home. The couple shares more of their life together, in and out of the home, as companions.

COMPANIONATE/EGALITARIAN MARRIAGE

Wife and husband are equal to each other, both are relational and independent, or either may be more one than the other, and both perform feminine and masculine roles in and out of the home. There's no difference in sex roles. Leadership and authority are completely shared. They relate to each other as close companions and partners in life. Both are primarily friends and companions to each other, joined in a mutually supportive and complementary relationship and sharing equally all familial tasks, responsibilities, and privileges.

Another way of looking at the variety in marital relationships is in terms of John Cuber and Peggy Harroff's five distinct life-styles: conflict-habituated, devitalized, passive-congenial, vital, and total. Couples may be quite stable in any of these five relationships. These do not indicate degrees of marital happiness of adjustment or permanence. An enduring marriage is not necessarily the same as a happy marriage. These types show different *kinds of adjustment* in marriage and different *ideas* of marriage. Just the mere *fact* of marriage, then, doesn't tell us about the kinds of experiences, fulfillments, and frustrations of the people who are married.

SPECIAL ISSUES IN MARRIAGE OVER TIME

CHOOSING A MATE

Getting together. Culture limits our choice somewhat to a pool of "eligibles," though not, of course, in any official way. Generally, "likes" marry: the informal pool of eligibles for a particular woman is made up of men of the same, or very close, race, nationality, age, religion, and socioeconomic class. How does a couple get together within this pool of eligible mates? They may encounter each other in either a close or a broad area of interaction, such as working together in the same small office (close) or as students at the same large university (broad). The size of the context in which they encounter each other has a great deal to do with the nature of their beginning relationship and the basis for the relationship initially. For example, working closely together in an office would give them an opportunity to get to know each other as professionals and perhaps also as whole persons. Their relationship would begin as co-workers sharing a fair amount of common interests through their work; then they might begin to date and subsequently develop a love relationship, based on knowing, respecting, and enjoying each other as persons. Students often get to know each other well from studying together in class, like each other, and begin to date as a result of this kind of close encounter.

On the other hand, students at a large university may encounter each other initially in passing on the campus, or at a dance, one becoming attracted to the other without knowing the name or anything about the person. The basis of the attraction is physical (appearance, dress, style) and aspects of the personality conveyed by body

movements. This attraction may motivate one to make
contact with the other. Any subsequent relationship
would involve getting to know each other from scratch,
during which the initial attraction might or might not be
maintained.

There are other ways of getting together, such as
through mutual friends or relatives.

> My minister and his wife, newlyweds, met in
> a marvelously unlikely way for our times. His
> grandparents urged him to come and meet "a
> wonderful Christian girl" in their church.
> Though very close to his grandparents, my
> minister wasn't convinced enough of their
> taste to rush right over and meet their choice
> for him. But when the couple did (dutifully)
> meet, amazingly and almost immediately the
> mysterious something clicked.

Developing the relationship. In all cases, a couple
spends at least some time getting to know each other,
each other's values (whether consciously or not), their
mutual sexual attraction, and especially experiencing
how their personalities interact in close encounter and
as a couple in relation to the rest of the world. We all
know how mysterious human relationships are—why
earlier or later in a relationship something works and
two people become a couple, develop their relationship
more or less intentionally, drift into or thoughtfully
choose marriage or live together without marriage for a
while, or break up.

The time together in a relationship is an opportunity
to get to know oneself and each other. The couple may
actually be strangers to each other, though "in love."
Their love may be based on ideal images, not real
selves. Over time in a relationship, they can learn to re-

spond to the other person rather than to a projection of an ideal girlfriend or boyfriend. However, they may retain idealized images of each other until the light of marriage's daily intimacy and responsibility exposes these as unrealistic, incomplete, or even false. Whenever this happens, the relationship must adjust to reality.

The relationship may also be an opportunity for self-discovery. Loving and being loved, especially for ourselves, opens us up to life and to our own potential. We may become more fully ourselves. We may discover capabilities or interests we never knew we had, or dare to develop new abilities. Love is very much like the role of the church in recognizing, affirming, and supporting the gifts for ministry of the people of God: the personhood and gifts of the beloved are recognized and enhanced by love. This self-discovery also includes the ability to recognize limitations and shortcomings, to change what can be changed and live with the rest.

Through both self-discovery and getting to know the partner in a relationship, the relationship and love may either deepen or die. This can happen either during courtship or after marriage.

PREMARITAL COUNSELING

While recognizing and even celebrating the mystery of love relationships, churches and even some states also know that sometimes love is blind and that the mystery of relationship always requires nurturance, understanding, and intentional work to be maintained in marriage. Thus, premarital counseling is a very common and valuable practice, sometimes even a requirement. Most churches specify at least one counseling session between the couple and the clergyperson before the wedding ceremony. Many offer or require much more substantial opportunities. Some provide premarital counseling on weekends for groups of couples. The Roman Catholic Church has a series of "Pre-Cana" conferences for engaged couples.

> A Seattle Protestant church provides a marriage counseling program, including a part-time staff person and a multisession course. All couples desiring to be married in the church pay the fee for the course, though their participation in it is voluntary. The program is thus supported financially, and most couples elect to take advantage of what they are already paying for.

Premarital counseling focuses on the education of couples in the economic, sexual, communication, child-related, work-related, and spiritual aspects of married life. Couples are led to articulate how they see each other, themselves, and marriage.

Many ministers, on principle, will not perform marriage ceremonies for couples who simply call up or come by and want to be married without further ado. They take seriously the church's theological and ethical understanding of marriage and its responsibility, assumed through the marriage service, and insist on premarital counseling for every couple asking to be married in the church. Some even require the couple to have an ongoing relationship with the church, believing that the choice of a religious ceremony of marriage assumes a relation with the church and that marriage (undertaken in the presence of the church) needs the continuing support of the church community.

The state of California pioneered in authorizing mandatory premarital counseling for young couples. The requirement developed out of experience in providing prenatal services, in which teenage women revealed their lack of health knowledge and their many problems in everyday living, and from data on the high percent of teenage marriages in the state resulting in divorce. Thus California required minors to participate in premarital counseling concerning social, economic, and personal responsibility within marriage, in the hope that this guidance would help to prevent or reduce future marital and family difficulties.

THE MYTH OF THE "RIGHT" MATE

Imbued with the romantic ideal of love portrayed by advertising and the media, we wait for the "right" man to come along or, as modern women, we go out looking for him. When we find this special person, we express the wonderful discovery that "we were made for each other." But in fact, there are probably hundreds of potential partners with whom we could build a good and close relationship, whom we could love. And the blissful romance with the joyfully discovered "right" man with whom we "fall in love" may not sustain a lifelong marriage relationship. Being in love is not the same as being loving, and it is the latter that undergirds and sustains marriage, not the glow of romance or the good fortune of finding "Mr. Right" and then simply drifting through life in a daze of happiness.

There can, of course, be a "wrong" mate, and many people who are wrong for each other fall in love. This is a case when love is blind. The couple, or one of them, may be more in love with love than with the partner. They may idealize each other, seeing each other superficially, not really knowing each other or even themselves but "loving" a partner who fits the current cultural ideal of beauty or fills a gap in their own personality. Fortunately, many of such couples fall out of love as they get to know each other through spending time together, perhaps during engagement and premarital counseling; others marry. Divorces may result, either from this illusion or from the illusion that the "right" mate ensures marital bliss—or at least a happy marriage.

The two important points here are that there isn't a uniquely right mate and that the right mate doesn't ensure a happy marriage. We do need to get to know each other, and especially to learn who we ourselves are, to be ourselves, and to share our real and whole self with our partner; and we need to *be* loving, intentionally, in the relationship with our mate. Choosing marriage and choosing a mate involve both these necessities.

BEGINNING TASKS OF MARRIAGE

A newly married couple has to work out their pattern of living together in the first weeks and months of marriage, consciously or unconsciously. Each has some notion of what it means to be a wife or a husband, based on their parents' marriages and those of others, peers and relatives they know well, as well as on cultural images of marriage they've absorbed. Ideally, they have talked over their ideas and ideals of married life, together and in premarital counseling, so that each knows what the other thinks and expects, and they have already begun adjusting those preconceived expectations to the reality of their own personalities, habits, and ideals. This may involve thoughtful intention *not* to duplicate the marriage pattern of their parents or others they know. These early weeks, then, involve becoming a *married* couple, getting to know each other more profoundly, developing a pattern of living together intimately in a unique relationship, and beginning to carry out a number of common tasks of marriage.

Some of the tasks of marriage include: working out satisfactory household routines and schedules that allow the couple to function smoothly in the home, at work, and during leisure-time activities; learning the cooperation required for living as an intimate pair; working out mutually satisfying and realistic systems for getting and spending the family income; achieving a satisfactory sexual relationship; developing competence in decision making; developing a communication system, especially ways of expressing and dealing with differences creatively; relating to community, friends, and relatives in their married status; developing satisfactory relationships with relatives, especially in-laws; and beginning to decide whether or not to have children and developing a readiness for parenthood. This list does not indicate *how* these tasks should be carried out in a new marriage, or even describe how couples actually do this. In fact, there is an enormous variety in married patterns of living. What is important to realize is that couples do develop their particular patterns early in their marriage; the question is whether the way they do so results in satisfaction and enjoyment in their married life together. Here, their communication system is crucial. While they are working out their way of living as an intimate pair dealing with these tasks, they are also developing their way of communicating with each other, about that process and everything else. An early pattern of open and accepting communication of feelings is invaluable. Through this, they will be able to take stock of their developing pattern of married life, share misgivings and unrealized expectations as well as satisfactions, and possibly adjust their way of life more in accordance with their mutual desires and less in accordance with unconscious sex roles, inherited marriage patterns, or social expectation.

But adjustment to living intimately with a spouse does take work. Even if each partner has lived with roommates before marriage, a spouse is a different and unique kind of roommate, and the adjustments typical of any joint living arrangement take on a much more powerful emotional importance when the roommate is your marriage partner!

Probably the two biggest adjustments and tasks of beginning marriage are the shift from courtship to marriage, from the relationship of a dating couple to that of a married couple, and the development of marital roles, becoming a wife or a husband and what that means. The first is an adjustment even for couples who have lived together before marriage. For some of these, marriage literally ruins a good relationship! And that's closely related to the second adjustment, to marital roles.

DEVELOPMENT OF THE RELATIONSHIP

The marriage relationship is developed over time, through different stages of life. It is affected by time and by factors both internal and external to the family.

Internal factors. Marriages are affected by children, housing, religion, health, and so on. *Children* change the marital relationship both between the partners and between the couple and the wider society. The marriage becomes different because of children. This is one of the changes that may be a point of growth and enrichment but may also result in less attention of the couple to each other and a drifting apart.

The kind of *housing* the couple lives in affects their marriage also, just as environment always affects whatever takes place within it. The amount of space regulates intimacy and tension level; the couple may spend time working on their apartment or house and yard; housing is an important part of the couple's regular expenditures; and the aesthetics of the housing, whether simple or elaborate, affects the pleasure of living.

Religion may have a strong influence on the marital relationship, positively or negatively. If it is a mixed marriage, religion may be divisive at some point; this may complicate in-law relations. There may be conflict if one partner is religious and the other not. Children add to this complication. Religion may affect family planning. Religion may also be an important part of the couple's life, with significant time spent at church and social life centered around church friends. The church may provide support for marriage through marriage enrichment courses, adult education, preaching, and counseling. And the religious faith of a couple may be the foundation of their relationship, in good times and bad.

Finally, *health* affects the marital relationship. We take good health for granted, but energy and vitality contribute to a good sex life and good spirits, and therefore to the relationship. Illness and hospitalization are costly financially and relationally. They are sources of worry and stress. They drain energy, so that relationship is more difficult. They disrupt sexual relations, at least temporarily. Despite these costs of illness, many couples weather them and support each other, being truly covenanted together in sickness and in health. In whatever way, however, health is one of the internal factors that influence the marital relationship.

External factors. What we usually think of as the private relationship of marriage is also affected by factors outside the home. Some of these external factors include jobs, the amount of money available, the family's location (usually determined by a job), friends, and possibly church and extended family and in-laws. Whether or not one or both partners are employed, what kind of work is done, and how much money the couple earns are three factors that have a tremendous influence on the marriage, regardless of the couple's basic love for each other. They affect self-respect, feelings of security, the time a couple has together, marital roles, family mobility or geographical stability, life-style, and even the kind of person each partner becomes. And these three factors are not simply a matter of free choice by the individual or couple together but are partly chance and largely determined by the state of the national economy. To a lesser extent, and in different ways, friends, church, and the wider family influence the relationship of the couple also, in either positive or negative ways or both. The church and the wider family are both internal and external to the marital relationship, being part of who we are as religious people and members of families but also outside the marriage as an institution in society and beyond the nuclear family.

We can see, then, that the kind of relationship enjoyed or suffered by a couple does not depend only on their feelings for each other but perhaps even more on other factors. The cost in divorce and family violence of national economic conditions, for example, is too seldom counted; instead, the family is blamed for its weakness and moral laxity. For those of us who are married, it helps at least to recognize that these additional influences are operating in our relationships and to talk about them together and with other friends who may have had similar experiences. This is especially valuable, within the circle of the community of faith, and all throughout marriage as these influences arise and before they gradually push our relationships with our husbands in an unnoticed and perhaps irrevocable direction.

Time. Change, however, is not bad in itself. Our marriage relationships do change over time as we move through different stages of our life cycle, and this change may be growth, one of the things most desirable in marriage. Some of the internal and external factors just mentioned are related to the life cycle, especially children and health but oftentimes jobs (and retirement) and location and others as well. Some of these have a cumulative influence over time; others change along the way (relocation, job loss, death of family members), thus bringing change into the marriage through time.

Having a child is one of the most important sources of change in a marriage. Earlier the couple changed from being a dating couple to being a married couple; now they adjust to being a married couple with a child (or children). This changes their relationship with each other and with society. These relationships change as the children grow up, especially in adolescence and then when they leave home. The couple may grow apart during the childbearing years. When children leave home or get older, the wife-mother may go to work outside the home, and this causes changes in the marital relationship. In mid-life, career demands may be great and distracting, or a mid-life crisis may bring great change. Retirement causes a different kind of change, as both partners are now at home and with leisure. Here the amount of money available is again an influential factor. So is the psychological factor of self-image and self-esteem as a nonworking person; this is especially significant for men. The marriage may undergo change as a couple tries to reestablish psychological intimacy after years of work distraction. Physiological changes through the life cycle also affect the marriage.

Companionate, partnership marriage involves mutuality, dialogue, renewal, and change over time. The partners grow as persons, and their relationship develops and deepens through dialogue and mutual support and challenge. They may change considerably as individuals; their relationship may accordingly be renewed. And marriage is *for* growth, for *life*.

A marriage, then, good or bad, does not remain the same from beginning to end. The relationship changes through time, influenced by many factors in and out of the family and by the life cycle.

SEXUAL RELATIONS IN MARRIAGE

Sexuality is a good gift of God, part of God's creation, and sexual relations are a very important dimension of intimate companionship, a part of the partnership of mutuality. Just as the rest of the marital relationship requires thoughtful development, so does the sexual dimension. And just as the rest of the relationship undergoes change and growth over time through the life cycle, so does the sexual aspect.

Sexual relations are both an expression of and a contribution to intimacy. Our sex life in marriage reflects the state of our relationship and helps to make the relationship what it is. Our sexual behavior with our partner comes to represent the whole relationship: sex can be strongly positive or strongly negative, depending on the dynamics of the larger relationship. With trust and intimacy, sex can be a powerful symbol of that closeness and increase it; if we are alienated from each other (and possibly others, ourselves, God, or life in general), sex may become a potent force for increasing that separation. When the general relationship is good, our sex life is likely to be mutually satisfying, reasonably frequent, varied. When we are angry, under a lot of stress, bored with each other, or the like, sex may be avoided as much as possible or be quick and unsatisfying or exploitative. On the other hand, of course, sex is sometimes the only good thing in a marriage, almost the only way a couple relates at all, or may be the means of reconciliation in anger or soothing of stress. And a reasonably satisfying sex life may hold a couple together and keep them working on their relationship.

A key point is that sexuality is not just physical or biological, and our bodies are not separate from our whole selves; we are whole beings and sexuality is part of the whole person. There is a wholeness of sexual response because of the integration of body, mind, and soul and our relatedness to our partner and community. Therefore, mechanical approaches to sex and sex thought of purely as physical betray the nature of the person and the nature of sexuality. Sex is much more than intercourse only, though it often includes that. Sex focused on genitals and orgasm only is inadequate; that's "making love with genitals instead of selves."

Sexual relations, then, are part of the goodness of marriage and of any alienation in the relationship.

The sexual relationship changes over time, from simultaneous unfamiliarity in the beginning (even if the couple has had sexual relations before marriage) and intensity and excitement, to a fairly established pattern that is generally satisfying, to a changed pattern when children come into the family or there are other changes in job or family or with illness, to perhaps renewed excitement and frequency around mid-life and when children leave home or post-menopause, and finally possibly some decrease in frequency and intensity of intercourse and/or orgasm or, for some couples, cessation of genital sexual relations but continued physical closeness and holding. When there are problems, this cycle may begin with fear of sexuality (often, unfortunately, related to religious faith and upbringing) or lack of knowledge and end with prejudice and misinformation about aging (an understanding that sex is for the young and is unhealthy, impossible, or undignified for the old, or that elders have no sexuality or sexual feelings or are physically unattractive). In between these poles may be misgiving about sexuality and the body, which can continue in the marriage and restrict the variety or frequency of sexual relations enjoyed by the couple. A partner may feel that some things are improper or perverted and that sexual relations are just a lower bodily neces-

sity compared with spiritual or intellectual things in life
and even the rest of the relationship. Very often, sexuality is associated with sin. The idea of sin itself has a
distinctly sexual connotation in the popular mind. It's no
wonder, then, that many people are uncomfortable with
sexual feelings or with talking about sex, even to a husband they're close to. In addition, many of us don't know
our own bodies—we don't know our anatomy and how
our sexual organs look, are made, and work. Or we feel
that our bodies are inadequate, especially in comparison with media promotion of female beauty and body
shape. In both cases we're alienated from our bodies,
and therefore from ourselves.

In a good intimate relationship, we may experience
the grace of acceptance of who we are, including our
bodies and our sexuality. Our bodies *work*; they are full
of life and feelings and *therefore* beautiful! We become
attuned to our bodies and all our feelings and celebrate
the life we experience in our bodies and our relationship. We can try any sexual activity that promises to be
fun and pleasurable or intimate and that does not hurt
either of the partners, so long as there is mutual agreement: and sexual relations can continue to bring pleasure and express closeness for a couple until death ends
their intimacy. This is especially so if an active sex life
is maintained throughout marriage, including resuming
sexual relations as soon after illness or separation as possible. There is no physical reason why active sexual relations should not continue until death; barring disease,
sexual capacity is lifelong. And it is life enhancing! Wonderful stories of active sex into the eighties and nine-
ties, including lusty desire and enjoyment and the be-
moaning of a decrease in frequency of intercourse to
"only three times a week in the last year or so," can in-
spire all of us and dispel any uneasiness we may have
about sexuality or any apprehension about old age. And

new knowledge about spinal cord injury and increased sensitivity to the reality that we are all sexual and continue to be, despite severe injury, has led recently to increased possibilities for sexual relations for spinal cord–injured persons; this can be lifesaving for them and their marriages.

Sexuality and some form of sexual expression are integral to our selfhood and our ways of relating. A satisfying sex life is essential for intimacy. Of course there are many ways of expressing sexuality, many kinds of sexual acts: an intimate glance or smile, a caress on the back of the head in passing, mutual masturbation, sensual caressing of palms and fingers or between the toes, intercourse, oral-genital lovemaking, kissing of the face and whole body, and so on. And there are many moods of lovemaking, from playful to erotic to tender; different lengths of time spent; different times of day and night. The two partners in a marriage do not necessarily have the same sexual needs or timing of sexual desire or interest. Further, outside factors affect the sex life (such as children, privacy, or work schedule). Therefore, continued attention to and open communication about the sexual part of a couple's married life is essential to intimacy. Problems can be talked about together and with medical and/or pastoral counselors. Helpful books are available, such as *Our Bodies, Ourselves,* Nelson's *Embodiment,* Comfort's *The Joy of Sex,* and the United Church of Christ study, *Human Sexuality.*

Though sex and sin are so commonly associated in our society, sex is *not* sin. The basic form of sexual sin lies in our *alienation* from our sexuality. Yet sex can indeed be a means for acting out our sin, and this good gift of God may be transformed into a burden or a weapon or a cynical game. Too often even the church acts as though marriage should be left alone in its private realm, once the church has blessed it, and assumes that any sexual act or other behavior is legitimate and the family's own affair once the church has legitimized the relationship with a marriage ceremony. But sexual sin may be acted out within as well as outside of marriage, causing great pain to some partners and severely harming the marital relationship. Christian witness against sin and offer of reconciliation should be made by the church in this instance as well as all others.

Sexuality may also be a means of knowing the grace of God and experiencing it, thus increasing and deepening our knowledge of God and ourselves. Sexuality may be one of the arenas through which the grace of God is expressed. In experiencing sexual wholeness, fulfillment, and love, we experience divine grace. Coming to accept and affirm our bodies, being reconciled with an alienated partner, and sharing deep physical and spiritual union in intimacy with a loved partner are such occasions.

CHAPTER 6

Self and Children

DECIDING TO HAVE CHILDREN

One of the greatest changes in family life ever to occur has taken place within our lifetime and that of our parents: Parenthood has become a choice. Though not completely so, of course, it is now possible for the great majority of people in our society to decide to have children or to decide *not* to, as well as *when*. Family planning is a realistic opportunity.

Before the present day, children arrived as a blessing or a burden, or they didn't; in either case, little intentional choice was involved, or at least little was effective. Having children was almost inevitable for married couples. Further, it was viewed in society and the church as one of the chief reasons (if not *the* reason) for marriage and one of its great blessings: sexuality was given humanity for the purpose of procreation; procreation almost automatically resulted from sexual relations; marriage existed to provide a legitimate context for sexual relations and the children that were produced. Therefore, society assumed that married couples would have children (and no one else would). It followed that because women obviously had the key role in procreation, society assumed that having children was one of their chief roles (if not *the* chief role), that women attained their deepest, most complete fulfillment in having children, and that no woman was complete without children.

As reliable methods of birth control were developed and family planning began to be feasible, this assumption still stood. Birth control was legitimized largely in terms of *spacing* children, not avoiding motherhood. Childless marriages were regarded as lacking an essential element and therefore were considered as pitiable or, when intentional, as deplorable. Up to the present, then, having children was inevitable or imperative.

Now, however, many radical changes have taken place.

- Having children is no longer inevitable: a realistic choice exists
- Motherhood is no longer viewed as the primary definition and role of women or as women's chief fulfillment
- It is more possible to overcome fertility problems and achieve conception
- Alternative ways to become parents are more common and accepted
- Parenthood is more available to single women and men
- Parental sex roles are more flexible
- Child day care as an alternative in child rearing is more available

Largely a matter of choice rather than circumstance nowadays, the decision to have a child—to become a mother—is one of the major decisions of our lives (along with marriage and work). And it is an irrevocable decision: you can't quit or resign from motherhood as you can from a job, or divorce your children as you can your husband (except for women who relinquish custody or give their children up for adoption). And in those relatively few cases where a father has custody, the mother is still mother of their children and usually sees them regularly or on occasion. This is certainly true of mothers whose children have been taken by the state because of allegedly poor care. The decision to have a child is a crucial one, affecting all the rest of your life.

Though not all married women now become mothers, most marriages do lead to parenthood. And probably for a majority of parents this experience is satisfying and fulfilling—in general!—though certainly not always *fun*. Rearing children is hard work, often nerve-racking, certainly very demanding and challenging, and irrevocable.

> A family joke in the Jacobson family, frequently asserted by Ellie in recognition of the heavy demands of parenthood and as her way of deflating the sentimental, idealized popular view of totally dedicated motherhood, is her statement, "Our marriage is very stable because I've told Bill that if we ever get divorced, *he* gets the children!"

MOTIVES FOR PARENTHOOD

What are the major reasons for having children? What considerations enter into this important life choice by couples and individuals?

Research on major motives for having children indicates the following:

> Altruism or unselfishness: nurturant, affectionate, and concerned parents
>
> Fatalism: parents feel an obligation to procreate
>
> Narcissism: child will look like parents or bring pride to parents

Masculine pride: "I made a baby!" "I'm a man!"

Instrumentality: child may serve some purpose (bring the marriage together, continue family line)

Conformity to pressures imposed by family and society: "When are you going to make us grandparents?" "All our friends have kids."

Role conformity: women's reason for being and fulfillment; proof of male virility and maturity as a provider

MOTIVES AGAINST PARENTHOOD

Motives for remaining child-free include the following considerations:

High cost of raising children

Overpopulation

Conditions in the world today: not fit for a child

Other fulfillment in lives: women have own lives, men are satisfied in career, couple is satisfied in relationship with each other

Reluctance of women to do two full-time jobs: mothering and career

Uncertainty about stability of marriage

Dislike of children

Unhappy childhood

Sometimes the decision about having children is painstakingly thought through and carried out.

> The Hills, a highly educated professional couple, were happy in their careers and their marriage and felt deep misgivings about sacrificing any part of their lives to have children. Paul, especially, feared risking the closeness of their marital relationship. As Joan neared the age of thirty-five, the couple talked

with a group of close friends in their church.
Most were parents and gave the Hills a hard
sell on behalf of parenthood, but Joan and
Paul got a dog instead! Two years later, however, having weighed all the considerations,
they finally decided to take the risk. Now both
are enthralled with tiny Paula and say they
could not have imagined the love they feel for
her and the increase in their closeness to each
other.

Some couples practice family planning rigorously.

Janet, a perfectionist, would hardly go near
her husband without putting in her dia-
phragm; they wanted time to adjust to their
marriage before having children. Two years
later, when they decided they were ready,
they practically wore themselves out during
the optimal week for conception, but they'd
been overconfident. Next month they followed all the rules even more painstakingly,
and this time Janet conceived, and their first
son was born.

Other times the decision is made by default: either the
wife gets pregnant unintentionally but the couple is at
least reconciled to the fact, or she doesn't conceive and
they don't take any special measures to have a child.

CONTINUING SOCIAL PRESSURE
Despite the choices available, society still expects
married couples to have children and there is social
pressure for conformity to this expectation. Some people
speak of couples without children as draft dodgers, evad-
ing their social responsibility. Despite widespread satisfaction in having children, the demands of child-rear-
ing are so substantial that many couples with children

feel ambivalent and therefore envy and even resent voluntarily childless couples.

This social pressure is magnified in the case of women. Many people, consciously or unconsciously, still hold the traditional view of women's role and women's source of fulfillment. It is this role that is asserted most forthrightly as the primary argument against equal rights for women: women are mothers; women stay home and care for children. Therefore, because of both the real demands of child rearing and this traditional role of women, married women in particular are resented when they exercise the choice not to become mothers.

> Sandra's sister illustrated women's attitudes toward their lot in life and especially women's role as mothers when she expressed her resentment at Sandra's decision not to have children with this outburst, "How *dare* you refuse to go through what the rest of us have had to do!"

Many people resent or are threatened by the increase in equality in marriage today: roles women are freed from and roles men are taking on in the home. Some associate the women's liberation movement and egalitarian sex roles with women's new freedom to choose not to be mothers.

> One Sunday afternoon Earline was out riding her horse while her husband was at home washing lunch dishes. Her mother-in-law murmured, "Maybe if Earline had a baby she'd learn what it means to be a wife."

WHEN AND HOW MANY?

If the decision about having children is positive, choice about parenthood also includes the possibility of deciding on timing, spacing, and number of children: when to have children, how close together, how many.

Timing and spacing. Most couples still have their first child within the first few years of marriage, allowing time to get to know each other, work on the beginning tasks of marriage, and build a solid relationship. Some older couples want to start having a family immediately. But an increasing number of people, particularly professionals, are waiting ten or more years. The point of decision is around the wife's thirty-fifth birthday, after which the statistical chance of birth defects increases.

This time line operates for single women as well. They realize that their opportunity to have a child is drawing to a close. They feel the significance of this period of their lives even if they do nothing more than recognize it, perhaps with some regret, and then go on with their living. Some single women who've been in a relationship with a man decide to marry, primarily because of their desire to have a child. Still others, especially professional women, consider artificial insemination; a few, impregnation by a friend without intention of marriage. And others decide to adopt. Usually some years pass before a woman—or a man—decides that having a child within marriage is unlikely and moves on to consider other alternatives.

For some people parenthood isn't an intentional choice but a by-product of the decision to get married—to a person who already has children, becoming a stepparent by virtue of becoming a spouse.

When to have a second child or subsequent children is the question of spacing. Many considerations enter in, such as the ages of parent(s), the development of the first child, the family's financial and geographical stability, professional stages of parents, available help with child care (nursery school, child day care, nearby relatives or friends), and how many children are desired.

> Jane took the responsibilities of parenthood very seriously and consulted her pediatrician about optimal spacing. He advised that children three years or so apart tended to fight, while 18 months seemed better. Jane says she and her husband followed this advice—and their boys never stopped fighting till they went off to college!

> Jeanne and George spaced their three children widely, over a twenty-year period. They wanted to raise each one individually and keep having a new baby to enjoy.

Number. How many children to have depends on most of the same questions considered in timing and spacing—financial ability to support a family and work-related considerations—and also on the family background of the parents. People from large families may clearly want or not want many children themselves. Both happy and unhappy childhoods may result in the desire for a large family. Number of children wanted is also influenced by people's images of the family.

> Jonathan and Sally had four children in seven years and are talking of more, though they are in their late 30s. Jonathan says, "There still aren't enough people around the dining room table."

Most couples today at least consider world overpopulation and scarcity of resources as they plan their families, and some limit themselves to one or two children to adhere to zero population growth. But there continue to be very large families of 10 or 12 children, some wealthy and some poor, both often resulting from religious opposition to the use of contraception. In some cases a large number of children results from more than one marriage. Finally, some adoptive families are quite large; there's always "room for one more."

> The Simpkins, Jones, and Allen families all have thirteen children, most adopted. They come from all parts of the world, and some have various handicaps. The Jones family includes four siblings from Asia, who increased the family from three children to seven in one day! The Simpkinses were adding to their family for twenty years.

For other adoptive families the cost of flying to another country to get a child, as required by some intercountry adoption programs, limits them to one or two children.

In all these choices—whether or not to have children, when, and how many—decisions very often are *not* made initially, of course, but rather nature takes its course, and people then decide what to do. Deciding not to have a child will involve either terminating the pregnancy or placing the baby for adoption.

ALTERNATIVE WAYS OF HAVING CHILDREN

Most children are conceived without difficulty, within marriage, and raised in that family. Mostly they're born in hospitals, but increasingly some are born at home or in birthing centers, attended by nurse-midwives and family members. For many it is a positive family experience and a more humane way of giving birth than in most hospital settings. Contingency plans for hospital delivery in the event of any problem are highly advisable. In both hospital and home births, prepared childbirth ("natural childbirth," the Lamaze method and others) makes the experience of birth an unforgettable event. As we tell our "birthing stories" over and over, they become part of our family lore, remembered by couples in intimate reminiscence and perhaps recited to the child on each birthday.

For other couples, fertility problems are a heavy psychological and emotional burden: much self-doubt (of femininity or masculinity), alienation from a body that "doesn't work right," sexual alienation from the necessity of using sex mechanically as a means to the desired end of conception, blame and bitterness toward each other over trying so hard and failing. But many couples are so determined to have children that they resort to fertility drugs, operations to correct blocked tubes, artificial insemination by husband or by donor, or *in vitro* fertilization. These new developments offer hope to thousands. These couples need sustained support from friends and very intentional communication with each other to keep their perspective straight through a process that may last for years. A sense of humor and caring about other things that matter outside themselves are enormous helps in avoiding obsession with infertility. There are emotional highs and lows if a pregnancy, finally achieved, miscarries. But elation and thankfulness for a long-awaited birth are also possible.

Some couples faced with fertility problems move quickly to consider adoption. Others come to it after all hopes for conception fail. But some couples and single people consider adoption as a means of having children even though they have no fertility problem. Some of these people are concerned with overpopulation, others care about children with handicapping conditions whom they could lovingly parent, and some want to enrich their families in ways impossible biologically, through interracial or international adoption. There is a significant difference in psychological approach to adoption among these different groups of prospective parents, especially as to whether adoption is regarded as a positive, desirable option or a last choice. Couples with fertility problems should face their disappointment frankly and over time. They need to share their feelings with each other, talk to others with similar experiences, and possibly consult a counselor. Some couples do not want to adopt because they want "a child of our own," one who looks like them, carries their genes; they don't feel they could really love an adopted child. Presently it is difficult to adopt a white, healthy infant; available children may be older, nonwhite, from countries other than the United States, and with some minor or major handicap. Some white couples find it difficult to think of one of these children as "theirs." If they do begin to talk about adoption, all these feelings must be aired and worked through.

Adoption agencies are generally very familiar with such feelings and experienced in helping couples with them and with deciding about adoption. Couples do not need to present a perfect picture, either of their marriage or of their assurance in approaching adoption. Agencies expect clients to be normal human beings and will help couples and single people recognize their motivations and the consequences of adoption in their lives. They also help people decide what kind of child, among those available, would be best for them.

> Our social worker was skilled in helping us think through our motivations for and the consequences of adopting a mixed racial child in our white family, especially with my southern background, and our justification for doing so

in light of opposition to such placements by some black social workers. Some people feel very vulnerable to and resentful of judgment of their fitness as parents by an adoption agency. We didn't feel this at all. Nevertheless, evidently some sense of being on the spot came through to our two sons: when the social worker came for the home visit, the nine-year-old welcomed her effusively, offered her cookies, and then in a burst of candor lifted the skirt of the sofa we were sitting on and confessed, "See? Here's the old cover! We had a new one put on top!" We *were* approved for adoption, and that son gave his baby sister her first bottle at home sitting on that same sofa.

Support is important in all these alternative ways of having children. There is abundant support for married couples, but single men receive very little help in becoming fathers. However, it is possible.

While a bank officer in New York, John adopted three Vietnamese boys and led the U.S. fund-raising for a Vietnamese orphanage. Now he runs a home for 200 street boys in Colombia. He is father to his own three adopted sons and these 200 more! Emotional support for his fathering has come from several U.S. orphanage support groups.

Single women receive a bit more support, either in adopting or when, as single mothers, they choose to keep their own child born outside marriage. It is a great help to have a friend to accompany them to childbirth classes and the hospital for delivery. And child day care and supportive churches are very important for a successful family life. Natural childbirth classes and experienced mothers are valued supports for expectant and new mothers. And a loved partner as support and coach during labor who shares the entire experience is now part of childbirth for many women.

In adoption, other adoptive families are the most help. They open their homes, tell you their experiences and doubts, joys and pains, warn you about obscure parasites doctors won't recognize and language problems of developmentally deprived children from overseas, listen to your doubts and tell you it's all right to decide not to adopt a child the agency offers but you just don't feel right with. You see in their families how adopted children grow up, how different races live in one family, how handicapped children help younger siblings, how grandparents respond to adoption.

> When we had decided firmly we wanted to adopt a mixed racial child, we wanted to prepare our sons. Before telling them of our adoption plans, we visited an interracial adoptive family. It was a wonderful, warm visit with these delightful folks. In the car going home, one of our sons asked, "Could *we* adopt kids like that?" And from then on they were part of our planning and waiting.

The church is also an invaluable support in adoption, as well as any other way of having children.

> In both our adoptions our churches were our foundation. During the worship service mourning Martin Luther King's assassination and celebrating his life, we whispered to each other our final decision to adopt one of Boston's 300 "waiting" black children as our third child. And in the service of our new daughter's baptism a year later, that strong support community gathered us close.

> During the Vietnam war we organized a

county-wide church fund-raising effort for Vietnamese orphanages as one small but life-affirming action we could take. When it became possible for us to adopt a Vietnamese child, this group gave us tremendous support and celebrated with us at his baptism service.

The church is an inclusive and loving support community for our adoptive interracial family.

EFFECTS OF PARENTHOOD ON LIFE

Parenthood is something special. Parents have knowledge and understanding from experience that nonparents don't. They also have special obligations, responsibilities, and prerogatives of their parental role. Parenthood is both positive and demanding. It has such a tremendous effect on our whole self and life that it is rightly called a crisis, whether planned or not. Little attention has been paid in scholarly work or church programs to "parental satisfaction" compared to the abundance of studies of "marital satisfaction" and "job satisfaction." Yet out of human concern for ourselves as parents as we undergo the tremendous changes of parenthood and continue to live as parents for years and years, and in recognition of the grave problem of child abuse in our society, we *should* consider the effect of parenthood on human life.

INCORPORATION
Parenthood entails the initiation of an intimate, primary relationship with a crucial responsibility. Parents must incorporate a new person into their existing life, into the family circle. In the case of a single parent, the family itself is initiated with the coming of the child, en-

tailing a totally new responsibility and way of life.

Changes necessitated by incorporating this new person include:

- Reorganization of economic patterns of earning and spending money
- New demands on each parent's space, time, and attention
- Readjustment of balance of power in the family
- Reestablishment of intimate relationships
- Decrease of leisure time for adult recreation and social life

With this incorporation, the parent necessarily becomes "a person for another," at least for a while, and this has a major effect on the parent's life. Parenthood can be a full-time job for some years. In the beginning, the demands can be overwhelming, even suffocating. A human life, utterly vulnerable, is totally dependent on you, twenty-four hours a day. Adoption of an older child involves different and special tasks of incorporation, often quite demanding for a period of time.

MARRIAGE

Marriage is two people and one relationship, but with the arrival of a child, the family increases by only one yet there are now three relationships (and, with additional children, even more). The lines of communication change, and the balance of power shifts. What might have been a marriage of egalitarian sex roles may now shift to traditional roles of wife/mother as primary child nurturer and husband/father as provider—and outsider. Though the decision to have a child is not infrequently made in hopes of strengthening a weak or unhappy marriage, children rarely make for added happiness between a husband and wife. In fact, parenthood can destroy marriage through conflict over differing parental values and skills and realignment of parental attention.

Effect on Sexual Relations. The presence of children inhibits the freedom of sexual expression and timing, requiring greater control over sexual activity and its limitation to times when the parents may be exhausted. The intimate sexual relationship must be reestablished.

Conversation. Similarly, the intimacy and leisure of conversation becomes limited between parents and may be focused almost exclusively on the child. The primary caregiver, usually the mother, may be desperate for adult talk, increasingly so with additional children: all day alone talking to toddlers! During early childhood, parents can talk relatively freely over the children's heads, but there are always interruptions and demands for attention. As children grow older, parental conversation will usually include them. So we often find ourselves saving up until bedtime huge topics we're eager to discuss—and then forgetting them or being much too tired to bring them up.

Leisure. Before parenthood, partners often spend much of their leisure time together, alone in some couple activity or in social life with friends. With children, leisure time decreases drastically, and social life changes (as we will see).

In sum, children may enrich, complicate, and stress marriage.

WORK

These new tasks of adjustment to parenthood may involve maternity or paternity leaves, a temporary shift to part-time work, or one partner's quitting work for at least a while. Though fathers are increasingly taking a larger role in child care, in the overwhelming number of cases it is still mothers who adapt their work to parenthood. If temporary adjustments can be arranged within the established personnel policies of the job, parenthood is not likely to have a negative effect on work immediately after the arrival of a child. Otherwise, a mother may have to quit her job with no assurance of getting it back. Some women remain out of the job market until their children enter school or longer; sometimes they find they cannot pick up where they left off because they haven't been able to keep up with developments in their field. Others may return to a different kind of job because it is more congenial to their life-style as a mother (flexible schedule, hours coincide with school day, no "take-home" work, less stress) or even because their interests have changed with motherhood. Work is affected by parenthood when the perspective of mother or father changes in light of having a child or of taking stock of family life in later years; other values may then take priority over the absolute demands of work and we may spend less time at work, say no to some things, or turn down a promotion or a move that would encroach on the family.

For mothers who do work outside the home, child day care is essential—but it is not available in anything like the amount needed. Such care may be in group day care centers, very often provided by churches (as shown by a recent National Council of Churches study by Eileen Lindner), or in licensed home settings or informal arrangements with friends, neighbors, or relatives. Some workplaces are now providing child care centers where parents can see their children during the day, eat lunch with them, and so on. For school-age children, after-school care is even more scarce and is usually arranged informally with neighbors or with baby-sitters coming to the home. Often these are "latch key" children who stay alone, possibly checking in with their mother by phone. Worry about children in the house alone after school affects mothers at work.

Occasionally one of the parents must stay home on a no-school snow day or to take a child to the doctor. Sometimes parents take time off to attend a parent-teacher conference or a school performance by their child. Usually, however, in any of these cases, it is the families who make the adjustments, mothers at work who absorb the worry or lose a day's pay if they have to stay home with a sick child; the employer doesn't suffer. Mothers' work *is* affected by children in some professions such as medicine or academic work: professors who are women with children write and publish less than their male colleagues who are fathers. Again, however, the primary effect is on these women's chances for promotion rather than on the university or student body. (Adopting an older child with some health, language, and cultural adjustment problems certainly affected the work of dissertation writing in my own case!)

At any rate, motherhood and employment are closely interrelated; about half of all mothers with children under five—and even more mothers of older children—are now in the labor force. Work is affected by motherhood at least to the extent that arrangements—often elaborate ones—must be made to continue working.

SOCIAL LIFE

Children affect social life, often strikingly. Parents are no longer free to spend their leisure time any way they choose or dash off somewhere spontaneously or stay out very late. They must arrange for child care and thus are restricted by availability and cost of baby-sitters and the need to plan ahead. How many of us have spent hours on the telephone trying to get a sitter—and then sometimes still had to flip a coin to see which spouse would get to go when no sitter could be found! And later, when children reach adolescence, we forgo going out in order to be home for their parties or dates.

Social life is also often centered around the children. Parents and children go to school events together or go out to eat as a family. And frequently a couple's social group changes: their friends increasingly become people with children, even the parents of their children's friends. Sometimes couples begin going to church when they have children and participate in parents groups, church suppers, or intergenerational New Year's Eve parties.

With children, time and energy for social life diminish. Often a family's time together is spent watching television at home. For single mothers, opportunity for social life is decreased, on the one hand, but on the other they may go out more with other single mothers and their children. Teenage mothers' biggest adjustment may be the radical change of their social life.

Having children seems to lead to greater participation in civic life. Parents of young children are more active in town and school affairs, giving leadership to voluntary associations and activities such as scouting.

EXTENDED FAMILY

When we become parents, we often are drawn into closer relationships with our extended families and spend social life or vacation time with them. Grandparents are eager to see their grandchildren and vice versa. Relationships that have been strained in young adulthood, perhaps by a disapproved marriage, may be mended by the coming of children. On the other hand, in a small number of cases, the adoption of a child, especially an interracial or intercountry adoption, may result in a breach in family relations for a short or long time.

Children often love to get together with cousins and hear stories of when Granddaddy or Great-Aunt Myrtie was little. Sometimes older children develop an interest in their family background and spend time tracing the family roots and talking with older members of the extended family.

Close relatives, usually a mother or sister, often come to help out when a new baby is born. Relatives may provide child care while parents work or stay with children when a couple goes away for an anniversary celebration. Sometimes a child has the treat of a special visit alone with grandparents or cousins out of town.

Today it is most common for the extended family to be dispersed over miles, so daily relationships are not possible. Some families, however, do live close by and see each other or talk by phone almost daily, and a few still have an extended family member—perhaps a grandmother or elderly uncle—living with them.

RELATING WITH OTHER INSTITUTIONS AND PEOPLE

Child raising is not merely an individual problem requiring individual solutions; it is both affected by social and economic structures of society and supported by sources beyond the immediate family. Though it may often seem so, raising a child is not isolated in the private realm of the nuclear family.

Among the ways society affects child rearing are the following:

- Values the family is immersed in
- Access to employment and therefore standard of living
- Racial climate, which determines whether it is a healthy, just, and safe environment for black,

other minority, and white children to grow up in
• Social services the family needs to function

Child rearing involves the family with other institutions
in society, such as hospitals and medical centers, day
care centers, schools, churches, libraries, and museums.
Besides these, children are related to people beyond the
nuclear family who help us with their nurturing, socialization, and education, a few offering direct help:

• Day care centers and school lectures or work-
shops
• Church parents' groups such as support groups
for single parents or parents of children with
learning disabilities
• Church courses in sex education or parenting for
peace and justice
• Mothers' coffees, with child care provided by
churches
• Shelters for battered women and children, providing literal safety
• Support groups for spouses and children of alcoholics
• Emergency food pantries or overnight sleeping
accommodation for homeless and hungry families

A very few voluntary associations organize people to
work directly for change in social structures and laws to
provide a better social context for children and their
families and to provide concrete support to families of
children with special needs.

So we do not have to raise children entirely on our
own. Having children links us to the larger social world,
and our social networks often contribute to their support.

PARENTAL AND SOCIAL VALUES

Especially influential on child raising are the social values that permeate our culture. The sources of these values are multiple, including religion, American democratic traditions, and business and advertising. Despite the seeming isolation of today's family, broad social values are strongly felt in every aspect of family life, and parents are often hard pressed to sustain their own values in raising their children. Mass media are especially powerful.

Churches are an important partner in value education. Parents and churches must explicitly teach their values to their children and show them the reasons behind those values. The support of other church families for ethical and religious values held by parents can reinforce their teaching in their own family. A fine example of an educational and ethical approach to family values over against society's values is Kathleen and James McGinnis's book *Parenting for Peace and Justice*, with its companion workbook.

A valuable organizational resource developed in recent years is the Family Cluster Movement (see Margaret M. Sawin, ed., *Hope for Families*). We cannot sustain our cherished-but-different ethical and religious values as isolated individual families. We need other families and church members with whom to discuss values consensus. We must be *conscious* of values and be intentional about value education in our families and the church, rather than allowing our children to learn their values unconsciously from implicit cultural messages.

Those of us who decide to have children soon find that love is not enough; we also need knowledge and insight and self-control. Bringing up a child is hard work. Often parents, especially mothers, feel alone and overburdened. We all need support from sources beyond ourselves, both spiritual and social, to weather the inevitable storms. But there is great joy and satisfaction in enabling the family to continue to the next generation.

CHILD ABUSE

VIOLENCE

Reported incidents of child abuse have increased since 1967, partly due to changes in the law, which removed liability from those who report abuse. There are between one and two million cases of child abuse each year in the United States. The overwhelming amount of this violence against children occurs within the family: most abused children are abused by a biological parent. Further, child abuse is a pattern of child rearing, not usually a single incident. Injuries from this violence may be so severe as to result in death. Studies have shown abusing parents to be a random cross-section sample of the general population: from all socioeconomic strata, all educational and intelligence levels, all sizes and types of communities, and most ethnic groups. Most abusing parents are in relatively stable marriages. Battered children and women are thus within Christian families as well as others, and abusing parents are included among church members and readers of this book.

For the very life of battered children, police and social agencies should be notified in the case of physical abuse. Many communities have shelters for battered women and children. And abusing parents are themselves organizing Parents Anonymous groups (similar to Alcoholics Anonymous) in which they can acknowledge their abusive pattern and get help in understanding and stopping it.

SEXUAL ABUSE

Sexual abuse of children is also prevalent. Thirty-eight percent of females and 10 percent of males will be sexually molested by the age of eighteen. At least 50 percent of all child sexual abuse occurs in the family as incestuous abuse.

Naming this reality in church and media, and publicizing the availability of crisis centers, begins to bring it out into the open, where both victim and offender can get help. Rape crisis centers, shelters for battered women and children, women's support groups, and many clergy help family members talk about these present or past problems.

It may be hard to recognize sexual abuse of children. It is distressing to think about and hard for children to reveal. Children's behavior may change radically (withdrawing or acting out), or they may ask not to be left alone with some family member. Sexually abused children lose their sense of self-worth, as they feel responsible for the abuse, bad about themselves, wanted only for sexual reasons, exploited, and helpless. Yet they are usually afraid to disclose the abuse, either because of threats by the abuser or the likelihood of not being believed. It is important to realize how unlikely it is for little children to lie about sexual abuse; therefore, if any child tries to tell us, verbally or nonverbally, about sexual abuse, we must pay attention and get help and protection.

It is a difficult problem for the nonabusing parent—usually the mother—in such situations to face and deal with also. She may not want to know it, may be physically afraid of the abuser or economically dependent, or may resent the child for disrupting the family; yet both the nonoffending parent and the sexually abused child need help and support in this serious difficulty. The same is true of adults who were sexually abused as children and have never been able to talk about their experience or confront their abuser.

The church could provide a crucial ministry to families involved in some form of child abuse and, in the process, serve the wider community. A United Church of Christ minister who directs the Seattle Center for the Prevention of Sexual and Domestic Violence, Marie Fortune, has contributed to this needed ministry through her work and her recent book, *Sexual Violence: The Unmentionable Sin,* which is a very helpful resource for churches, families, and women's and men's groups.

CHILDREN AND ADULTS WHO ARE NOT THEIR PARENTS

Many of us have children in our lives who aren't our own. We are related to children as stepparents, foster parents, grandparents, godparents, extended family members, and special friends.

Becoming a *stepparent* by marrying someone with children may be a bonus or a cost of that marriage. The role of not-quite-parent may be difficult for both stepparent and stepchild, especially complicated in a combined family of two sets of children from previous marriages where each partner is stepparent to the other's children.

Foster parents relate as transition family to children of a range of ages for long or short periods of time, giving and often receiving love, as well as laboring mightily and sometimes with frustration. Many children, especially teenagers, are not available for adoption but need long-term foster care.

The relationship of *grandparents* to the children of their children varies from very close emotionally and geographically to very distant in our highly mobile and

complex society. Some of us long to have grandchildren, and some badger their children (this is difficult for all grown-up children and especially for gay and
lesbian young adults, who are pressured to marry for this
reason). Others feel threatened by the prospects of
becoming grandparents. Letters, calls, and pictures become the primary means of relating with distant grandchildren. Divorce is difficult for grandparents' continuing relationship with grandchildren; many grandparents
try to keep up the relationship regardless of custody arrangements. In relating to grandchildren, some may feel
more relaxed than in raising their own children and enjoy them more, especially because they go home after a
while! Both grandparents will probably be working for
years during the grandchildren's growing up and no
longer be available to stay with them or have them for
the summer as in earlier generations. At any rate, this relationship changes through the years as grandchildren
grow and change and grandparents age; there may be
both joys and disappointments in this process, as with
our own children.

Finally, we often relate to certain children as *god-
parent, relative, or special friend.* Many single people
enjoy such relationships in families and thus have children in their lives in a very meaningful way. They spend
holidays with the family, invite the child for visits, and
keep up close communication over years. Godparents
may maintain similar close relationships. In church, single adults, elders, and married people with children may
have special relationships with children in the congregation. The same is true of youth. The church thus becomes extended family, and the entire church family is
linked with all others within God's creation.

In this book we have tried to look at family life as a
religious commitment to develop a relationship holy in

God's sight, a partnership that contributes to abundant life for each family member and for God's world. God calls us to a love for the whole of humanity. Family and church thus mutually seek to develop a vision of the global interdependent human family and to live toward inclusive community. We build *koinonia*—Christian community—among ourselves within families and the church, based on just and caring relationships. And we extend this koinonia by acting in the world for a new creation in human relationships and society—a new order of justice, community, love, and human wholeness.

Bibliography

Ariès, Philippe. "The Family and the City." *Daedalus,* Spring 1974.

Boston Women's Health Book Collective. *Our Bodies, Ourselves,* rev. 2nd ed. Simon & Schuster, 1976.

Chafetz, Janet S. *Masculine-Feminine or Human?* 2nd ed. F. E. Peacock, Publishers, 1978.

Comfort, Alex, ed. *The Joy of Sex.* Simon & Schuster, 1974.

Cuber, John, and Peggy Harroff. "Five Types of Marriage." In Arlene S. and Jerome H. Skolnick, eds. *Family in Transition: Rethinking Marriage, Sexuality, Child Rearing, and Family Organization.* Little, Brown & Co., 1971.

Farley, Margaret A. "New Patterns of Relationship." *Theological Studies,* December 1975.

Fortune, Marie M. *Sexual Violence: The Unmentionable Sin: An Ethical and Pastoral Perspective.* Pilgrim Press, 1983.

Fullerton, Gail Putney. *Survival in Marriage: Introduction to Family Interaction, Conflicts, and Alternatives,* 2nd ed. Dryden Press, 1977.

Harrison, Beverly, and James Harrison. "Some Problems for Normative Christian Family Ethics." *American Society of Christian Ethics Selected Papers,* 1977.

Jourard, Sidney. "Marriage Is for Life." *Journal of Marriage and Family Counseling,* July 1975.

Lindner, Eileen, et al. *When Churches Mind the Children.* High Scope Press, 1983.

McGinnis, Kathleen, and James McGinnis. *Parenting for Peace and Justice.* Orbis Books, 1981.

Nelson, James B. *Embodiment: An Approach to Sexuality and Christian Theology.* Augsburg Publishing House, 1979.

Rogers, Carl. *Becoming Partners: Marriage and Its Alternatives.* Delacorte Press, 1972.

Safilios-Rothschild, Constantina, ed. *Toward a Sociology of Women.* Xerox College Publishing, 1972.

Sawin, Margaret M., ed. *Hope for Families.* William H. Sadlier, 1982.

Shonick, Helen. "Pre-Marital Counseling: Three Years' Experience of a Unique Service." In Jerald Savells and Lawrence Cross, eds., *The Changing Family: Making Way for Tomorrow.* Holt, Rinehart & Winston, 1978.

United Church of Christ. *Human Sexuality: A Preliminary Study.* Pilgrim Press, 1977.

World Council of Churches. Ecumenical Prayer Cycle. Geneva, 1983.

———. *Jesus Christ, the Life of the World: Worship Book for the Sixth Assembly.* Geneva, 1983.

Yates, Wilson. "The Family: A New Pluralism and a New Wholeness." *Theological Markings,* Spring 1982.

———. "The Family and Power: Towards an Ethic of Family Social Responsibility." *Annual of the Society of Christian Ethics,* 1981.

———. "The Future of the Family: The Family of the Future." National Council of Churches Workshop, Ecumenical Event, November 1981.